Food, Sex

&

Peace of Mind

Food, Sex & Peace of Mind

(What A Woman Needs To Know To Keep A Man)

Author: Chey B.

This book is written as a source of motivation and inspiration. The content of this

book has been carefully researched in efforts to ensure accuracy. The author and

publisher assume no responsibility for any losses, damages, or injuries incurred as a

result of applying the information provided in this book. All practice of the included

information should be carefully studied and clearly understood before taking any

action based on the contents of this book.

AskCheyB P.O. Box 380846

Brooklyn, NY 11238

Visit our website at www.askcheyb.com

Library of Congress Cataloging-in-Publication Data is available upon request.

ISBN: 978-0-9884258-0-4

Printed in the United States of America

Photography by @HottShotzPhotos www.hottshotzphotos.com

Book Cover by @Jbdesigns1

Editing by @SoniaCarroll

First Printing: December 2012 10 9 8 7 6 5 4 3 2 1

Food, Sex

&

Peace of Mind

(What A Woman Needs To Know To Keep A Man)

Chey B.

This book is dedicated to all the women who desire to be loved, valued, and appreciated by a man. I hope this book will help you to work towards becoming the best woman you can be so that you may attract the best man. To my dear son Ethan, already I see greatness in you. May you grow to be the great man of honor I am raising you to be, and treat every person (man or woman) with love, dignity and respect.

Introduction

With Wisdom Comes "Understanding"

One thing we as people have in common is that we all want to be loved. We don't always know how to receive it, and after we've been hurt a few times, it seems as though we sometimes don't know how to give it. If you've never had a broken heart, you can't possibly be human. The good book says that love is patient, kind, and long suffering, but we tend to forget about the "long suffering" part.

This life we live is a blessing. We are not meant to stay here on this earth, we're simply passing through, so while we're here, we must enjoy the life we have, and live with a purpose. Life is about building relationships and leaving behind legacies, so while you're doing all this walking, talking, and breathing, don't forget to *live*. *You* are the common denominator of every relationship you are a part of; 50% of your relationship success will depend on *your* "relationship readiness", the other 50% will depend on the readiness of your partner.

A common mistake that many people make is they seek love from others before they find love within themselves. You'll have more love to give if you're the harvester of it; it's impossible to give out something you are without. One should never stop being in a relationship; even when you're single, you should always be in a relationship with yourself and with God. Better people attract better people, so before seeking out a relationship with someone else, make sure you've fallen deeply in love with yourself and are at your best.

It's true that you are who you attract; once you take the time to get to know yourself and love yourself, you will then discover whom you really are. Depending on who you are at that present moment in your life, you are likely to attract someone who embodies similar characteristics. If by chance, you find yourself at your *worst*, then that would be the best time to take a step back from others and build a stronger relationship with yourself.

Being "relationship ready" is essential to the success of the relationships you start and will heavily influence how or why your relationships end. Temporary satisfaction only lasts until you get bored; overcome yourself, get bored with that, and *then* challenge yourself by taking on a relationship with someone else. Always begin with the end in mind; instead of dating endlessly and aimlessly, figure out what you want from your life and what you want out of him, and then come up with a plan, set goals, and create an ideal timeline for which you want these things to come into fruition.

With any great relationship comes great planning; you have to want it badly enough for it to be successful and last forever. When you think about it, building a relationship is all about *strategy*, but don't play yourself by trying to outdo or outsmart those who are playing on the same team as you. When you're in a relationship, it's no longer about how *I* can win, but how *we* can win together. Be completely transparent and bring both parties strengths and weaknesses to the table. Once everything is on the table, you both can come together as a team, and share responsibility based on one another's strengths and be a force to be reckoned with.

Without good communication, there will be misunderstandings, and with that comes an emotional disconnect which inevitably leads to a downward spiral of problems in your relationship. In addition, if you're speaking to your partner in a way that he's not receiving well, not understanding, or not responding to, that can prove to be just as ineffective if not more than not communicating at all, because words have power even if the receiver isn't responding to them.

Men and women communicate differently, and value different things, so if your desire is to be with a man, you'll first have to understand *you*, then you'll have to learn to understand *him*. So often, I hear women complain about a man who constantly references her body; that same woman would later complain about how the man she's stuck with *now* isn't compliment her at all. *Attraction* is of extreme importance when choosing a mate, so instead of being offended by his adoration of your physical appearance, learn to love it. Men are motivated by food, sex, and peace of mind, and the more he can look forward to it, the more he'll be motivated to work for it.

Ladies, when a man shows interest in anything you have, that's your opportunity to scope him out. Determine whether or not he's worthy of your time, and then sit down at the negotiation table (i.e. A date.) Everyone knows that a woman likes to be complimented, catered to, appreciated, and treated well. Well I've got news for you; men like those very same things, and it's not very often that we get it, which is

Food, Sex & Peace of Mind

why we refer to that special lady as "The One". The "one" is someone who takes the time to learn, understand, and appreciate a man; someone who is interested in growing *together*.

How well you understand a man will show in everything you do; men rarely communicate their thoughts and feelings through words, but rather through actions. A man will speak less when he's happy and satisfied, and he will show you just how much he loves and appreciates you through his actions. You'll hear a man speak more when something's not right! He'll use words to bring attention to messages his actions didn't convey. And that's the sole purpose of this book; to enlighten and empower women to put their best foot forward so that the right man will come into their lives and move forward with them. The content found within these pages are designed to help put the way men feel about women and relationships into actual words.

A man will do anything just for the opportunity to sleep with a woman, so getting a man will almost never be a problem for you. *Keeping* a man however will require a great deal of strategic planning matched with understanding what motivates a man to settle down. Knowing what motivates him to commit will be the key you'll need to unlock the door to a monogamous relationship! The subtitle "What A Woman Needs To Know To Keep A Man" isn't to discredit you for what you already know, but rather to give you a deeper look at the way men think from the mind of a thinking man. With wisdom comes understanding!

A relationship between two people takes hard work and dedication, but with strength, courage, and wisdom and Faith, any and all things are possible. If you're looking to be in a relationship that's easy, stay single! Even then you will run into problems on a "single person's" levels. What a relationship does is it gives you a foundation, a support system, a blanket to help cover you when you're cold and alone. You may think you know men, but how well do you understand men?

Chapter One

Get To Know Yourself

Finding True Love

Life is about building relationships and leaving behind legacies. Before you can have a happy, healthy relationship with someone else, you have to establish a happy, healthy relationship with yourself (spiritually, emotionally, physically, and financially). When you focus on being the best person you can be, you'll attract the best people. It's important that you take as much time as you need to focus on yourself before focusing on another individual. Be independent when you're single and interdependent when you're in a relationship. Being independent is one of the keys to having relationship success with someone else; it shows that you are very well capable of taking care of yourself with or without a man.

Being in a relationship means that you're getting ready to combine your resources and become *one* with one another! If you want the best results for your relationships, it's best that you first find yourself, and gain independence before getting involved. Finding yourself will require you to distance yourself from certain people and things, and take a spiritual journey, in hopes of finding your own way! Taking a spiritual journey will help you see value in yourself, people, and all of the things available to you on this earth. Often times, we take for granted the people and things that are readily available to us, and we sometimes forget that we are all worthy of love, honor, and respect.

When you take the time to focus on yourself, you gain a new appreciation for your time, energy, and effort. The things you do for yourself will be the standard for what the man who comes into your life must do. Take as much time as you need on this

2

spiritual journey and seek a true understanding of what love is and what it feels like. Once you've identified with what love is for yourself... Enjoy it to the fullest!

Learn ways to open yourself up to both giving and receiving this divine gift! A spiritual journey is best when experienced alone so that you can develop the strength, courage, and wisdom you'll need in the face of adversity. Being able to depend on *you* will come in great handy whenever someone you love decides to walk in or out of your life! Without faith, your relationship(s) will be limited to only what you are physically able to do with your senses.

Faith is having hope for something that is not in your power to control, and believing in your heart that it will come into fruition. Having a sense of spirituality brings you closer to you, and closer to a higher power. Believing in a higher power humbles you and helps you stay grounded, no matter how highly favored you may be in society. Faith cannot be complete without logic and reason; you want to hope for the best, but also have enough sense to know when you're dealing with a lost cause.

Before you can become the Queen in a man's castle, you have to prove that you can be a humble servant. A woman who shows that she can be submissive is more likely to attract a man who has the desire to be a leader, protector, and provider in her life. Men are very simple; we have our pride and we have our ego, and all we ask is that you stroke it every once in a while. You'll come to find that a man will do exactly what you want him to do, if only you can make him feel as though it was *his* idea. It's a small price to pay for a happy, healthy relationship, but it's well worth it in the end.

A man needs to find *himself* before finding a woman, but when he's finally ready to settle down, he's going to look for a woman who can add value to the life he's built for himself. The woman he's looking for is someone who offers something that he's missing; he needs a match, not a duplicate! A man of substance won't want or need you to pay his bills, protect him against the threats of the world, etc., because he's already got that covered. What he wants from a woman is love and nurturing A.K.A. sex, food, and peace of mind! Yes, these things are quite easy to produce, however they should only be given to a man who's proven himself worthy of these privileges.

If you're already giving a man sex, cooking, cleaning, and not getting on his nerves, he'll already feel as if the two of you are married. The only problem is he's not your husband. This man is getting all of the benefits of a marriage without the ring, the wedding, and the covenant. Again, men are very simple; we can go an entire lifetime living with a woman, sleeping with a woman, and just "hanging out" with a woman without ever taking things further. By respecting yourself, and making marriage a pre-requisite for sex, you'll establish what will be a mutually beneficial arrangement and a mutual respect between you and your partner.

Sex is something that a man you're not married to should be able to look forward to, not look back upon. The man you're dealing with should know that you're interested in more than sex before having sex. Once you give a man sex, you give up your negotiating power! You should always set standards and requirements for a man to meet, in order for him to have sex with you (i.e. Marriage). A man will do anything for the chance to have sex with a woman, and marriage is no different, so don't be afraid to make this a requirement whenever you're propositioned for a place in your life or your bed.

Love has no reason, it has no bias, and it flows any and everywhere, and has no conditions. When you find someone you love, you will feel it in your heart, however having feelings for someone is only half the battle. Getting to know a man will help you measure whether or not these feelings are mutual. A man knows when a woman is in love with him, however reciprocating these feelings to her will depend on his current position in life. If you ever come to find that a man is not emotionally, financially, or spiritually ready to receive you, you should take heed, take a step back, and get back to focusing not on him, but on you!

Sex is a great way to keep a man in your bed, but it's no way to keep a man in your life. A man does not associate sex with love, and he is almost always prepared to give his body to a woman simply for momentary satisfaction. Never confuse a man's lust with love because a man categorizes the two totally separately. When a man is looking for sex, he primarily uses his eyes; when a man is looking for love, he primarily uses his heart.

You will meet many men who don't see the value in being in a serious, monogamous relationship, but don't let that discourage you from being patient and waiting on the one man who does. Take all of your experiences from the men in your past, and use them as an example of the type of man you do and do not want in your life in the future. Throughout life, you will experience heartbreak and naturally, it will take some time to heal. Never allow the hurt from your previous relationship to prevent you from opening yourself up to a new relationship. Once you stop loving, you'll start hating and once you stop hating, you'll start loving.

When you allow yourself to dwell in misery over a failed relationship, you give the person who hurt you power over your life. The best way to take this power back is by forgiving them and moving on with your life. Nothing hurts a man more than being left by a woman, so if your relationship doesn't work out, do what's best for you and your life. Any hurt and pain that was inflicted by a man in your past relationship will hurt him more when he sees that you've left and never came back.

We all reserve the right to be happy, loved, valued, and appreciated, so associate yourself with people who offer these things to your life. Not every man you meet will be a candidate for marriage; however everyone has value and can serve a purpose in your life. Before writing a man off, create a list of categories, and place each man where you feel he belongs. These men can and will serve their purpose in your life, just so long as you're able to also add value to their lives in some way. If you're a woman of substance looking for a man of substance, present yourself as such.

It's essential that you show a man your heart before showing him your body; men will always be attracted to a woman's body, however sex will blind a man from love. When you show a man your heart from the beginning, it will attract men who are looking for substance. A man wants to have the impression that you know how to care of yourself and others; this is a great indication that you are capable of potentially caring for him. If you show a man your body from the beginning, you'll attract a man who's interested in sex, and it will be too late for you to show him your heart because he will no longer be interested or listening.

When it comes to matters of love, you should love yourself and love everyone else, no matter what their relation is to you. Always treat others with the same dignity and respect you would like given to you. Never allow a man to be your only source of love, because a man can up and leave you at any given moment in time. If you can find love and happiness inside of yourself, you'll never go a day without it. If you're looking for love, hold up a mirror!

Be Emotionally Available

Being in a relationship requires that two people share their worlds with one another. You share your mind, body, resources, and more in order to help one another grow as a couple. In order to attract the best person that will fit into your life, you first have to work on *being* the best person you can be on the inside and outside. When you love yourself, the positive energy that you possess inside will shine through and rub off on everyone around you.

The last thing you want to do is give off a vibe that's not warm and welcoming, because you'll repel more people than you attract. Hate is a repellent, but love is a magnet. Use love as a tool to attract people both in your personal and professional life! Often times, when we're lost, we'll search to no end for love in all the wrong places (i.e. Food, drugs/alcohol, sex, etc.). Instead of searching outwardly for sources of love, search within for sources of love. Once you start to value and appreciate yourself, you'll be able to both open yourself up to love and be loved by someone else.

When you find love and happiness within yourself, you can set the standards for what you expect to receive from the men who come into your life. When you're in doubt of a man's love, you can always refer back to self and ask, "Is he treating me the way I like to be treated?" When you solely rely on an outward source for love, that love does not belong to you; the power lies within that source. If the direct source of love isn't within you, it will be impossible for it to be readily available whenever you need it.

If lord forbid, your sole source of love were to die, abandon you, or abuse its power, you'll find yourself extremely vulnerable to heartbreak and pain. By loving yourself, your source of love/power lies within you and will never die, leave you, or forsake you! Make loving yourself an everyday regimen for the rest of your life. Wake up in the morning loving the way you feel, look in the mirror loving the way you look, and finally, be open and prepared to love the rest of the world!

Loving yourself is an inside job that starts at home. If love dwells in your home, you'll be more careful with who you let in it, you'll cherish/protect it, and your heart will always have a place to revive itself whenever in need. Your home is your place of peace, your escape from the world, and your comfort zone. The things you place inside should be people and things that bring you love, joy, and happiness (i.e. Family, music, pictures, food, interior design, fragrances, etc.). If the world and the people in it treat you cruelly, you'll always have a place to go as a reminder of what love & happiness feels like.

As tempting as it may be to stay home and embellish in all the goodness that this "love environment" has to offer, remember to spread love to others once you find it in yourself. Finding yourself and loving yourself is a journey. For many, finding love will require redefining what *love* is as a whole; this may be due to severe emotional damage caused by previous distributors of love in the past (i.e. Parents, former lovers, friends, etc.). Love is something that you do and feel; once love is felt and then exchanged, it becomes evident that they are *in* love with one another. Love feels good; you'll know you're not in love with someone when it hurts you more than it makes you happy.

Anytime something you've associated with love becomes detrimental to your health, it needs to be removed from your life. When you remove someone or something from your life that hurts, you leave more room for someone or something to come into your life that helps. You have to love yourself before you can love someone else. Having love for yourself, as well as others immediately adds value to your life and the lives of others, which in turn establishes your worth to the men who want to be in your life.

You will come across many people who will try to convince you of what loves means to them, but becoming emotionally available and finding yourself means you're not looking for others. Being emotionally available is about being in love with yourself so that you can open yourself up to loving someone else in the future (by your standards). Often times, we look for love in all the wrong places and overlook the one place love should always be found… in ourselves! When we lose sight of the foundation of love, it's time to take a step back and pay more attention to what's most important in this world… "You!".

On this journey, you want to figure out what feels, looks, tastes, smells, and sounds good to *you*. Avoid any influences who don't have your best interest at heart; use this time primarily to enjoy being alone and figuring out what's best for you and your life. Throughout life, you will come across many people who will intentionally hurt; even people you thought may have loved you. Not everyone who's in your life wants the best for your life. Even people you've lived with, shared secrets with, shared the most precious years of your life with will have a hand in your heartbreak and disappointment over the years. By removing this pain from your heart, you're allowing room for pleasure to come in. Pain will only remain in your heart for as long as you give power to its source.

If something is causing you to be unhappy, locate the source, eliminate it, and reclaim your power. You can take away any and all power from its source by *forgiving* others for any pain they've caused you. By clearing your conscience, you take away all unhappy thoughts and forgive the people who caused you to be unhappy. Love & happiness is a magnet! People are attracted to those who appear to be happy either because it reminds them of themselves or of where they would like to be.

Friendship is the key to building up romance; romance has the potential to lead to a committed relationship; a committed relationship has the potential to lead to a lifelong commitment (i.e. Marriage). In order to establish a true friendship with someone, there has to first be love and happiness inside of you that attracts them. If your inner beauty is dimmed, your outer beauty will be the only thing left to shine. Your outer beauty is what will get a man to come; your inner beauty is what will get a man to stay.

Continue to work on being the best person you can be, and you'll attract the best people. Being emotionally available means that you're ready to love and be loved by someone else. Always remember that relationships aren't for everybody; relationships are only for the ready. Repair and restore your heart before making it available to someone else. If someone you love doesn't know how to take care of your heart, learn

Food, Sex & Peace of Mind

your lesson and stop giving it to them.

Know Your Worth

Men of substance love women who exude confidence in themselves. It shows in the way you walk, dress, speak, the words you choose, the places you go, the people you associate with, etc. No matter whether a man is looking for a quick lay or someone he can potentially grow with, he will look for these qualities to assess how he feels *you* feel about yourself. After his initial assessment (if he chooses to approach you), he will treat you according to whatever analysis that he came up with.

There are times where a man will find a woman to be extremely attractive; meanwhile *she* doesn't have a clue what it is about herself that attracted him in the first place. This is an example of having low self-esteem and not knowing your worth. There's a girl I went to college with... She (hands down) was the most beautiful girl at the school, and all of the guys agreed and would say great things about her. However, *she* didn't have a clue just how beautiful she was, nor did she believe that she was greatly desired by any of the men on campus. At the time she was a "20 year old virgin".

She's gorgeous, has a great physique, is very intelligent, she graduated with honors and is doing very well for herself career wise. She has no kids, has never been married, has great morals, values, and excellent character. Sounds like a dream girl doesn't it? Sure, she's great! But in order for her to be considered by a man, *she* has to know and believe that she's valuable. It doesn't matter if all the men in the world realize this... If *she* doesn't realize her worth and portray herself as the beautiful/intelligent/accomplished woman that she is, she'll run into men who are likely to try and take advantage of her current state of mind. A man of substance won't even want to be bothered because there's no challenge.

Being in a relationship with a woman who has low self-esteem will feel like a burden to him because she'll constantly be dependent on him for validation. Instead of her looking in the mirror and evaluating her own self-worth, she will look to the man who saw value in her. Or worse, she'll outsource and seek approval from men who have nothing invested in her. A man of substance is completely turned off by women who try too hard to get attention from men, and she falls to the bottom of the list of marriage potentials.

Every day when you wake up, you have to evaluate yourself before presenting yourself to the world. For example: In the morning, you go to the bathroom, brush your teeth; making sure that your teeth are nice and clean so that when you smile in the mirror you'll be the first to validate your million dollar smile. If you feel good about smiling at yourself, you'll feel great about smiling at others because you know that you did a good job working on it. Now you can walk out the door with confidence, knowing that the people you're smiling at are seeing exactly what you saw when you looked at yourself in the mirror. The most important person to impress in life is you!

If you've looked in the mirror and have realistically evaluated the person you are inside and out, you will either like what you see or you won't. If you don't like what you see, you'll at least know what you need to work on to make yourself feel more confident and to raise your self-worth. Remember, you're doing this because you feel a certain way about your image, not because of how someone else feels about your image. As adults, we are all held accountable for *self.* So continue to focus on yourself and on being the best person you can be.

When you're the best person you can be, the people affiliated with you will have no choice but to either take it or leave it. If they don't like the person you are when you're at your best, then you're probably not the right woman for them. <<< And that's ok. You only need one man to settle down with, so never mind the rest. The ones who aren't interested in you aren't the right man for you either. So don't think you're less valuable simply because you've got all of these things going for yourself and the man you're interested in still doesn't want you. We all reserve the right to be selective. And we all individually select people to be in our lives based on how we feel about ourselves and how we feel about the other person.

Remember, the way you view and present yourself is the way people will ultimately view you. No matter what image you think you're portraying, the heart of your presentation will shine through every time. If after you evaluate yourself, you decide that you like what you see, you can be confident in knowing that even if the people of the world do not see you as someone valuable, that *you* see you as valuable. And the people who are interested will approach you based on your inner and outer beauty.

Evaluate yourself every day and love the person that you see. Once you love what you see, your esteem and your confidence will automatically boost, and the energy you put out will be so great that others will begin to notice. Remember... you're not evaluating yourself just so that men will notice you. You're evaluating yourself so that you will know within yourself that you are worth noticing. Being pursued by men is only one of the many rewards you'll inherit by simply holding yourself to high esteem and being confident in yourself. The greatest reward is being comfortable in your own skin.

Once you're comfortable in your own skin, the men will want to rub up against it. Raising your self-esteem and confidence raises your worth (your value). Once you possess something that you know and believe is of value, your next step is figuring out how you're going to market it. Anyone who is potentially interested in investing will consider you based on the market price you've set for yourself. But you first have to evaluate yourself so that you can determine your self-worth. Self-worth is great if you plan on being alone, but when you know your worth, you also have to show your worth if you want to be considered for a relationship/marriage. Your worth is determined by the value you add to the lives of others! But it starts with you!

Be A Priority, Not A Convenience!

Everyone in this world has value; we are all worthy of being happy, healthy, and prosperous. Often times we sell ourselves short and never achieve greatness because we don't believe in our own hearts that we are worthy or that we can do it. This fear of *yourself* will keep you on the ground, as opposed to elevating you to new heights. If you will settle for less, people will give you less; if you will settle for more, people will give you more. Things that are convenient in life often have high frequency visits because gaining access doesn't require much work. There's nothing wrong with being a convenience to someone, just so long as the arrangement is mutually beneficial.

Once a convenience becomes an inconvenience for you, it's time to re-evaluate your position in that relationship, require more, or position yourself in a more beneficial relationship. Place value on your time, energy, effort, money, and resources; not everyone who's around your circle needs to be in your circle. When it comes to building relationships, it's essential that you set your own personal goals for your life, and with each person you meet, you give them a place in your life depending on whether or not they are in alignment with your goals.

Without a plan, without goals, without any idea of what you want your relationship to be like in the future, you will inevitably find yourself settling for whatever/whoever is most comfortable at the moment. If you want your relationship to be a success in the end, you have to have a successful beginning. Always begin with the end in mind. There are billions of men in this world, and you only need "one"; you don't have to accept just anyone, you can develop a plan of action and get exactly what you need from a significant other.

Key word *significant*! Your significant other is someone who is worth mentioning, someone you're proud to be with, someone you're looking forward to growing with. When it comes to someone who is merely a convenience, you can barely see past the end of the month with this person, let alone a lifetime. This is your life we're talking about, and you're not getting any younger; every day you live your life should be lived with purpose. When it comes to people you give your time to, you should add people who add value to your life, and subtract the people who don't.

As you continue to grow as a person, your values and your priorities will change, and so will your desire to associate with certain individuals. Depending on your current position in life, you may feel as though a *convenience* is exactly what you need. That person who agrees to be a convenience more than likely feels the exact same way about you. The only problem with that is the foundation of your relationship is not build on anything solid; the foundation of a convenience is based on temporary short-term satisfaction which doesn't last.

Once one or both parties find themselves, and develop love for themselves, they will no longer need you. Finding the "perfect match" isn't about finding someone who has the same exact thing you have; finding a match is about finding someone who can produce something your life is *missing*. The last thing you want to be missing from your life is love and happiness because it's impossible to give out something you are without. If your source for love and happiness dwells in someone else, then you'll be left unfulfilled if that person is a) unavailable or b) decides to leave you.

You are worth more than a quick lay and a brief stay; there is someone out there who will love, cherish, honor, and be loyal to you, and you won't have to share him with anyone. You have to believe in your heart that you are worthy of greatness; the way you prove this is by disassociating yourself from failures. Once you change your heart, you will change your mind, which will prompt you to make better choices for your life and your relationships. The key is to have Faith and believe that God knows your heart, he knows the work you need to do on yourself, and he knows the type of man you need in order to achieve relationship success. #GodIsLove

Men are simple and only require Food, Sex & Peace of Mind; if you give this to a man, you will certainly have no problem keeping him around. But that's not the end; keeping him around is merely a *convenience*. Now that you know what makes *him* happy, you need to sit down at the table and negotiate before any "goods" are distributed. A man will do ANYTHING for the opportunity to sleep with a woman; with this in mind, you need to take this opportunity to set standards and requirements, otherwise you will fall in the trap of being his convenience.

Your vagina is your negotiating power! Once you give a man your body, you no longer have any room to negotiate, and you'll be stuck giving this man food, sex & peace of mind, trying to figure out "What am I doing wrong? I'm giving him everything a man needs, but he's not giving me what I need... How can I fix this?" It's too late! You are now officially his *convenience* because you did too much too soon. Sex is the ultimate goal for a man, so if you give it to him on day one, you'll be lucky if you see him on day two (especially if the sex was bad). Even if the sex was bad, he may give you a call just to feel something wet and warm, but he won't have much more use for you outside of the bedroom.

Men are very simple and do not require much; but *you*, you're a female and you want the WORLD! A man can sleep with multiple different women 7 days a week with no emotional attachment, and no desire for any type of future whatsoever. Don't get your little heart broken trying to play a man's game; don't get yourself caught up in the convenience trap. If you want more than Food, Sex & Peace of Mind, then you need to require it, otherwise, men will continue to take you for a test drive until you're completely out of miles, and then move right along to the next.

It's important to have actual conversations about short-term and long-term goals, just to see how a person feels about their life and to see where they plan on going in the future. A man knows the role he wants a woman to play in his life before he even meets her. Getting to know someone properly is essential to relationship success and it will help you to differentiate what is suspense and what is *substance*. Instead of allowing someone to treat you like a convenience, give your time to someone who will treat you like a priority. You are worth it!

Let Go of Fear

We have a limited amount of time to live on this earth and leave our mark on the world. We're born, we're raised, we live our lives, and then we die leaving behind memories that hopefully keep our spirits alive. There's only but so much a person can do within 100 years, but it's exciting to see all that we can aspire to accomplish during this time. Your purpose here on this earth isn't to live only for self or to fulfill the pleasures of a man, No! Your purpose is to spread love and do it more abundantly!

Fear is something we all face at some point in our lives and it sometimes prevents us from reaching our fullest potential. You may find yourself being afraid to let a man get close to you after you've had your heart broken. You might be afraid of losing your job; a job that you hate anyway, but need it to pay your bills. You may even find yourself being afraid of stepping out in the world on your own and gaining your independence. Fear can place a roadblock right between you and your destiny, and it's up to you to believe in yourself, face your fears, and overcome them.

No one is perfect so it's ok to get out there, take a chance, experience life, and even make mistakes while you're at it. Feel free to use your family, your friends, and the people of the world as your guide and learn from their experiences. A fool learns solely from his own experiences; the wise learn from that and the experiences of others. Getting insight from others can prevent you from experiencing certain things you'll be more than happy to avoid. Always keep an open mind and welcome those who offer insight that could be beneficial to your life.

There are so many places to go, so many people to meet, so many things to see and they're all within your grasp. All you have to do is simply believe that you can achieve it. If you desire to be married to a loving, honest, respectable man who protects and provides for you, you can certainly make it a reality if you work towards that goal. If you desire to have a family and travel the world, this too is achievable if you set goals and set out to achieve them. One thing is for certain though; it's impossible to achieve your goals if you don't set any!

If you want to travel the world, stop making excuses for why you can't, and start figuring out a way that you can. If you want to have a husband and a family, let go of your fear of being hurt by someone else and be open to loving again! If you want to become an entrepreneur and take control of your finances, don't be afraid to invest in yourself and be the best at what you do. There's no one in this world that can stop you from being your own boss, traveling the world, and having a loving husband and family to tag along for the ride. The only thing standing in your way is you!

Before you know it, this short life will be over, you'll look back on your accomplishments, and you want to be able to say "I am happy with the way I lived my life!" That's what life is all about... building relationships and leaving behind legacies! If you're miserable at the job you're working at now, let go of your fear and come up with a way to gain your freedom! If you're in a relationship that doesn't make you happy, free yourself, explore the world on your own, and be willing to open yourself back up to the new possibilities of love. If you're unhappy with the neighborhood you're living in, decide what your ideal location is, plan an exit strategy, and then get up and MOVE!

Before all of this advanced technology existed, there was just people, plants, and wild life; now we have tall sky scrapers, planes flying in the sky, cars driving on the roads, computers, cell phones, you name it. All of these things came to existence because someone, somewhere had a vision, and they took the steps they needed to make it a reality. Steve Jobs is one of the most influential men who lived in our time; he's no longer with us, but because of the decisions he made with his life, he made a difference in the world that will live forever. Steve Jobs didn't have anything that's not available to you or anyone else in the world. What Steve Jobs did was he let go of fear, and sought out to do something that no one else in the world had ever done.

This too can be you! You can create a blueprint for your life and for your relationships, and you can build upon it day by day until you've yielded your perceived results. Success is measured by one's ability to reach his/her goals, so if you want to be successful, set goals and work towards making your dreams a reality. Don't allow your life to pass you by, and be left with nothing to show for it; believe in yourself, make the best of your life, and be proud of your accomplishments.

Many times we are our worst enemies! The only thing holding you back from leaving a terrible relationship, a terrible job, or a terrible living situation is you! It's time to let go of fear and start living for the moment! Open your heart, open your mind, and get ready to explore everything this world has to offer. The sky is the limit, so let go of your fears and get ready for success in your personal and professional life.

Master *"The Look"*

Naturally, you are free to do whatever it is you want to do. But... there will be two totally different outcomes if you a) Approach a man you're interested in or b) Be patient and wait for the man you're interested in to come to you. Men are hunters! We like to chase, we like to conquer, and we like a challenge. It's actually fun for us guys to build up the courage to go and speak to a woman in ambiguous situations; not knowing whether or not we have a chance.

It's a thrill being turned down because (for men) this is all a game and it's a learning experience. Believe me; he will not be heartbroken just because he got turned down. He will be disappointed (at most), but he will live. He will use his brain to evaluate what just happened, and then challenge himself to figure out a better way to approach you the next time, or to approach a different woman from a different angle.

Whether or not he is successful in his approach with you, he still wants to be the aggressor & the initiator in order for it to be fun/interesting/exciting (for him). When a man is approaching a woman, he's not yet sure how interested she is in him (if she's even interested at all). That's the exciting part! That's what intrigues us! The *mystery* of it all! This is what's going to motivate a guy to try to figure you out and get to know you better... the fact that your feelings towards him are partially ambiguous. Partially ambiguous by no means insists that you're "not interested". All you're doing (as the woman) is downplaying your interest in him so that he'll be motivated to go harder to bring that interest out of you. #Seduction

If/when you're in the mood to start dating; you

should act as if you have multiple options, so when a man approaches you, your energy should portray that "this" (men approaching you) is something that you're used to. So no matter how interested you are in that man, try not to give off this "I'm super interested" vibe. You can tell your girlfriends just how "super interested" you are in him as soon as he walks away. But don't let the guy who's approaching you know (through your energy) that you are ready/willing/available/too interested in him because once he knows for sure; he will take you for granted.

You've got to keep this new stranger on his toes and wondering "Is she interested? Is she not interested? I can't tell, but I certainly want to talk to her more and find out." In fact, this is something you should do throughout your entire relationship/marriage. Keep things somewhat "ambiguous". But with your ambiguity, be sure to keep things honest. Once you get set into a routine, you get bored! Once you get bored, you look for excitement! Sometimes people look for excitement from their partner... and others (unfortunately) outsource. So keep things somewhat ambiguous in your relationship and try not to get set in a routine; and stay true.

Example: You know you want to have sex with your husband... but instead you roll over, close your eyes, and pretend you're sleeping. He then is motivated to try to take on the challenge of waking you up for sex. In his mind... you're sleeping. In your mind, you're challenging him to be the aggressor!! This is equivalent to a woman giving a man "The Look" (so to speak) so that he will be the aggressor, take charge, and go in for the kill. He gets the sex he was longing for and you get the sex you were longing for (that he had no idea you were longing for). And all you had to do was lay there. See how this works?

Here we talk about "The Look":

If you're interested in a man, all you have to do is give him "the look". "The look" is a signal that lets a man know that you're approachable and could be potentially interested in him. After receiving the look, he needs to come over to you, introduce himself, and find out what that look was about. If the guy does not take the bait... meaning he doesn't make a move when you give him "the look", then that means there is something stopping him from making a move. Now don't automatically think that he didn't approach you solely because he's not interested in you. There could be a multitude of reasons why he didn't approach you at that particular moment.

Here are a few examples: He could be married or in a relationship, someone who knows his partner could be present, he could be involved with someone or escorted someone who is actually there at the venue (just not currently by his side and he doesn't want to be rude), he could be shy and is not used to approaching women, he could be gay, or at worst, he could simply not be interested in you! No matter what his reasoning for not approaching you is, you have to accept the fact that he did not choose to entertain you... and you have to learn how to take a loss! You might see him again at another event and he might be single then... he might come alone... he might not want to miss another opportunity to approach you. So if/when you see him again, simply give him that same "look". By giving him that look (again) it will seem a bit more evident that you at least want him to come over and talk to you (if nothing else).

If during the first encounter you are so impatient that you can't stand the fact of this guy not making a move that you decide to make a move first, you may be running the risk of being negatively categorized or publicly humiliated. If he's not interested in you, you run the risk of embarrassing yourself in front of this man who you really like because for one... you're a woman approaching a man (which is foreign to him), and two, he's not interested in you! What's worst is you'll still have to be in his presence until you decide to leave the venue (which will be very awkward for you). Spare yourself!

By approaching a man, you eliminate any and all ambiguity! Now it's crystal clear (for him) that you are in fact interested in him. He no longer has to hunt because his prey came right to him! The *fun* is gone! The *chase* is over! The *game* is over!

So now, he's got you right where he wants you like a dead carcass ready to be carried away. He knows that you are interested/ready/available whenever he calls, so you will be that one girl he doesn't have to put forth much time/energy/effort with. He can just call you when he's bored or when all of his more challenging options fell through because he knows that you'll be available. He knows you will be there just waiting for him to reach out to you because you showed just how eager you were from the beginning. Just watch him after you're done approaching him.

He'll be sweeping the crowd looking for a real challenge (because you certainly weren't it). Even if he was interested in you at first, you've taken away his desire because you've taken on a male role by being the aggressor, and that's *his* position. The worst part is he's then going to talk about you to all his friends saying, "Man... you wouldn't believe what happened to me tonight! This "woman" just approached me!!! I'm going to have her wrapped right around my fingers!"

Being approached by a woman is only flattering to a man who doesn't have any options and isn't used to getting quality women. Don't think for one second that because you're drop dead gorgeous that a man will be impressed by you approaching him. No!!! You approaching a man will do nothing but boost his male ego. Your approach will have him thinking, "Damn! Am I really that fine? WOW!"

He'll also think that you're desperate, impatient, lonely, or are dying to get a man in your life. With these thoughts in mind, you will be the very last person he will consider for a relationship. At most, he will only consider you for friendship with benefits... All because of the way you presented yourself. Ask celebrities what they call women who approach them: "GROUPIES!" And for the average male, you approaching him will have that same effect. You will be the equivalent of a groupie and he won't respect you!

Now there are *some* men who will be flattered by being approached by a woman (i.e. the nerd, the geek, the older gentlemen, the jobless man, the man who has no swag, the man with no goals/aspirations, the man who has absolutely nothing going for himself). Oh *he* would love to be approached by a woman. But guess what? This isn't the man you want and you know it! So if you want a man who is of substance, then act like a woman of substance, and show him your worth by simply giving him a look that encourages an invitation.

Enjoy the fruits of being a woman! Men live for the hunt! All you have to do is give a guy "the look", and then sit back... relax... and watch the men come to you. By you approaching a man, it suggests that you lack confidence in yourself, you're impatient, and that you're not willing to take a loss. These are internal issues that can be worked on and will make you a more attractive woman for yourself and others. Always present yourself as a woman of substance; one who has confidence and esteem and you'll attract men who have those same qualities.

Chapter Two

Single by Design

It's Ok To Be Single

Before you can be a couple, you first have to learn how to be *single*! If being a couple doesn't work out, you will be right back where you started... *single*! There's no way of getting out of being single from the start, but the way you live your single life will certainly have an impact on the quality of your relationship with someone in the end. When you're a couple, there are "two" people to consider; when you're single, there's only *you* to consider, however, your consideration for others (while single) is an essential key to attracting a quality mate.

Your physical appearance will get a man to come, but the heart behind your outer beauty is what will get a man to stay. Add substance to your relationship by *being* a person who has substance. Being single will allow you the space and opportunity to focus on who's most important in your life (you)! Once your life, health, and strength is gone, *you* are gone, so put "you" at the top of your list of priorities before any other person. It's ok to love others endlessly, but never put an end to loving yourself.

A relationship without love is a relationship that is destined for failure. Love is the moral fiber that keeps a relationship together, so if love has not been added, whatever is hindering love's presence should be subtracted. When your relationship is guided by love, you'll be able to discern who is right from who is wrong for your life. It's not difficult to tell when a person loves you and when they don't, you simply have to acknowledge and respect the signs. Give it a test run on yourself; begin to do things out of love (for yourself) and then use yourself as the standard for which you will allow others to treat you.

With any and every relationship, there has to be an end goal in mind, and when it comes to being single, the end goal for you should be finding love and happiness *inside* of you and having the ability to share it with others. If love and happiness can be found inside of you, you'll never go a day without it. Having this independence puts you in preparation to live a happy, healthy single life until you are ready for something *more*! The idea is for you to continue to grow as a person, and as a people, so once you've found love inside of you, don't be selfish, spread it to someone else!

We often times go into relationships simply as a safety net or a comfort zone; relying heavily on our partner to deliver what we should've already been handling. Jumping into a relationship that you're not ready for is a disaster waiting to happen because there's no *end* goal in mind; the focus is merely on the right here and the right now. There will be more to eat when everyone brings something to the table. If your heart is empty, and you're looking to be filled by your partner, that leaves *you* full from what your partner is giving, meanwhile your *partner* is empty because you're not equally reciprocating. It's impossible to give out something you are without.

Before you start worrying about who, when, where, why, how you're going to meet the love of your life… BE the love of your life. The idea is to find a "match"; your match will be the person who loves you in the way that *you* love you and beyond. With this in mind, you want to build yourself up to becoming someone who is worth loving, having, and keeping. We all have a past, and there's nothing we can do to change it. Our past is who we *were*, not who we *are*; who we *are,* is the person we've become *after* experiencing our past. With this in mind, don't hesitate to totally reinvent yourself and present yourself not as you were, but who you aspire to be.

Often times we go our entire lives doing things wrong, and since we've been doing it for so long, we've totally convinced ourselves that it's right! If you've been doing something for years and it hasn't had an increase in growth or prosperity, there needs to be a *change* (If growth and prosperity is what you seek). No longer should you look at being single as something to avoid or be ashamed of; being single is something that you should embrace if that's where you are in your life. Being in a relationship or a marriage is for people who want and/or have planned for that life, but until then, enjoy your single life!

Being single is the thing you do when you're establishing/finding yourself and/or when you haven't yet met someone who meets your standards. The "right time" to be in a relationship or marriage is the time that's comfortable for you. Being in a relationship or marriage is an indication that you are ready, willing, and able to commit yourself to sharing your world with someone else. If you're not ready to make that commitment, it is A-Ok; relationships aren't for everybody, relationships are only for the *ready*!

Marriage is forever, so if you have the desire to be married, finding love within yourself while you are single is the very first step. If you want to be in any type of relationship of substance, finding love within yourself is the very first step. The idea behind being single is to reflect on "you" as an individual and an independent; take as much time as you need to figure yourself out before you dedicate your time, energy, effort, heart, and money to someone else.

Once you have established yourself spiritually, financially, and emotionally, your esteem will soar to new heights, your confidence will shine through in everything you do, and the love inside of you will beam onto everyone in your presence. Now that you've found love within yourself, you're a different person; you've changed your heart, which is changing your mind. You'll find that the way *you* make yourself feel, surpasses that of many people you've had in your inner circle, which will prompt an immediate "clean up" of your social network and surrounding influences.

Now that you've found love within yourself, you will want to surround yourself with people who are also ready, able, and willing to love you just as much, if not more! Your values system will change and your interests will be in things that inspire and motivate you to be better, which will introduce you to better people. When you're a better person, you'll be exposed to better options. When you're at the worst, the worst will tend to be more attracted, so your "singledom" needs to be a strategic design that is meant to elevate your standards of living.

Once you've learned to embrace being an independent and have embraced the art of being a cheerful giver of love, you are now ready to welcome *interdependence. Now* you have something more to offer, because you are giving what you have and what you can afford to give. You are no longer an empty heart looking to be filled by the next person you meet.

Food, Sex & Peace of Mind

You are giving what you hope to receive; you are leading by example; you are giving from the heart, and that's the best place to store your gifts.

Single by design is the "plan of action" you carry out when you are looking for growth and change. Some people are single because their partner broke up with them, some are single because they can't find a man, some are single because they ruined the relationship they had. These are all examples of "Single by default". You want to be "Single by design"; single by design means you planned to be single (not to be confused with lonely). Being single doesn't mean that you shouldn't interact with the opposite sex; single by design means that the main focus of your interaction should be with "you".

Never allow another person or other people to decide when the right time is for "you" to commit to someone. Only *you* should make that decision, and you should follow your heart. Before you use your heart, make sure your heart is in the right place; keep your heart above your waist where it belongs. Once your heart, mind, and spirit are in the right place, it will be much easier to find someone who is on the same page as you. Focus on your heart, mind, and spirit until it's *matured*. Focus on others when they too have matured, and have made the choice to focus on *you*!

Presentation Is Everything

Some say "never judge a book by its cover", but it's the cover that stimulates a viewer's heart, mind, and soul and prompts an approach. If the cover doesn't effectively give an accurate idea of what's on the inside, the presenter should come up with a better presentation. Who you are, where you're from, and what you're capable of doing counts for nothing if no one else knows it. And besides, we live in a visually oriented society, so the first assessment a person will make of you will be based on what their eyes can see. With this in mind, always present yourself in the way you want people to know and remember you.

An impression is the mark you leave behind after you've presented yourself. The first impression gives others an idea of the shape of your character. No matter how many times you try to make a new impression, the very first one you make will always be set in the hearts and minds of the people you've encountered. Many would argue "I don't care what other people think about me!", but the opinions of others should matter to you simply for the sake of your own dignity, and also because you never know who a person is, what they do, or how they can change your life. The way others feel about you can and will influence the favor in which they show you in the future, or the lack thereof.

The world is a center stage where we are constantly expected to perform. Being physically appealing attracts romantic admirers, being an intellectual attracts thought leaders and inquisitive minds; being loving attracts those who have love for you and/or seek love for themselves through you. The same effect is true of those who portray themselves in a less honorable or respectable way. It may be safe for you to step out of character in the comfort of your own home, but when you're amongst members of society, everyone should be able to recognize who you are (to them). The people around you should see something in you that they love and admire, as opposed to something that they hate and despise.

Men and women view the world differently; some women are heavily influenced by males in the early stages of their lives, which influence their male tendencies growing up. Some males experience the same thing, growing up amongst female influences, which in turn raise their female tendencies. For the average male, life is simple; everything is either logical or practical, and everything else outside of that is simply ambiguous. When a man sees a woman who dresses and carries herself like a whore, he initially fixes his mind to treat her like a whore. When a man sees a woman who dresses and carries herself like a lady, he initially fixes his mind to treat her like a lady.

We are all free to walk, talk, dress, and behave in any way that we choose, but it's important to consider the affect your actions have on others if you plan on closely associating with them in the future. A woman's outer beauty can gain the keys to a man's bedroom; a woman's inner beauty can gain the keys to a man's heart. If you are an exceptionally beautiful woman on the outside, it would be in your best interest to subtly portray your outer appearance and let your heart shine through. When a man is looking for sex, he closes his heart and opens his eyes. When a man is looking for love, he uses his eyes *and* opens his heart.

When you present yourself as a lady, you practice playing a role for the character that you want people to know and remember you as. In addition, you'll attract more gentlemen because you're exactly the type of woman a man of substance would want to settle down with. You'll avoid the unqualified men because they don't have the time, interest, or money to invest in a lady. These types of men are looking for a woman who carries herself like everything short of a lady, and who will accept short-term payments as opposed to long-term investments in her.

A man knows the role he wants for a woman to play in his life before he even meets her. If you present yourself as a sex symbol, he will want to keep you only as a sex slave. And once a man views you as a potential sex slave, he will no longer consider you for a serious long-term commitment. He will instead keep you around only at his convenience while he continues his search to find himself, as well as a more respectable lady. You have to be careful when you find someone who's a "perfect match". A whore is the perfect match for a pimp. A lady is the perfect match for a gentleman. Find yourself first, and figure out who you are, then when a man finds you, you'll be able to see whether or not he's a match for the woman you are.

It's best to always present yourself as someone who is worth knowing and worthy of a commitment. One of the many benefits of companionship is the access it gives you to another person's world. You go from being independent to being interdependent; sharing each other spiritually, emotionally, financially, and physically. Sex will always be a missing link in an individual's life because it's meant to be experienced

Food, Sex & Peace of Mind

with another person. Anyone who has the proper functioning tools below the belt can have sex; however it's the depth inside of you that will motivate others to want to remain a part of your life before and after sex.

Character can be detected through your eyes, facial expressions, word choice, style of dress, the company you keep, the places you go, the things you do, the overall way you treat yourself and others, etc. These are all reflections of who you are and what you represent. It's important that you always put your best foot forward because a man will categorize you based on your character before you even introduce yourself. A man can very easily measure whether or not your morals, values, and character are in alignment with theirs simply by sitting back and observing you.

People often use *words* as a way to seduce, to convince, and to sway an audience into believing something that benefits them. Their words appear to be reassuring, but often times are a lot less accurate than their actions. When a person wants to assess who you are and what you're about, they won't ask you, they'll watch you. They'll close their ears so that they're not manipulated by the impression you might have of yourself. They'll open their eyes so that they can see for themselves who you really are, and open their heart so that they'll know how your actions make them feel. Remember these principles when you're presenting yourself and evaluating others. When a person shows you who they are… believe them.

Let A Man Down Easily

Almost everything a man does in life is to please women; he gets a job, buys nice things, stays fit and well groomed, etc. all to impress a woman. There is no greater pleasure for a man than to succeed with a woman, and he'll go to any extent to get her. No matter how low or high the rejection rate may be, a man will never give up on a woman. Women change their minds depending on whichever way the wind blows, and men know this about you. If you don't already know this about yourself, make a note of it; since you're liable to change your mind at any given time, it's in your best interest not to burn bridges that you may want to walk across in the future.

You don't have to be romantically interested in a man to remain associated with him, and you have nothing to lose from keeping him in your circle. What you gain though is the respect of an admirer simply because you took the time to acknowledge him and entertain a friendly conversation. Kindness and compassion can help you both in your personal and professional life; after all, you never know who a person is, what they do, or how they can change your life, so treat every person you meet with dignity and respect, even if you have nothing invested in them.

If you are a woman who's at the very least physically appealing, admirers will constantly be knocking at your door trying to "get in". There's always a position to be filled, so keep all of your applications on file just in case. You never know when you'll need a personal trainer, a chef, a web designer, a photographer, a mechanic, a promoter, a DJ, etc., but it's great to know that you not only have one on file, but also that this individual has an interest in you and is likely to be motivated to assist you in any way possible.

Sometimes, the only "fees" required are simply that you make a man feel as though he's are a part of your life. Signs of gratitude and appreciation go a long way with a man, especially if he's not mutually benefitting from aiding you. When a man shows interest in you, this is evidence that he sees you as someone of value, and that he is in your life on his own accord. These are the types of individuals you want on your team for love and support whenever you need it. The last thing you want is for your circle of friends to be filled with people who don't actually want to be there.

SIDE NOTE: Go where you are celebrated! Leave the men who don't celebrate you to themselves.

There's a myth going around that "There are no good men left". On the contrary, there's an infinite amount of good men left. The problem in most cases is that women have a particular type of guy in mind, and a good man doesn't land at the top of that list. In fact, you can find plenty of good men if you rummage through the long list of men you've placed in the "Friendship Zone". Many women won't admit this, but most good men don't offer the challenge they need to keep them interested. She prefers a man who's a bad boy who she can potentially turn into a good man!

Whether you're attracted or not, as a woman of character, you should be kind to others because of who *you* are, not because of who *they* are. You will come across many admirers, who you're simply not attracted to romantically, and that's fine; we all have the right to be selective. Be clear from the beginning where you stand, but remember to always treat people with dignity and respect, and be honest in your approach. Treating others with dignity and respect has nothing to do with being interested; it's a simple matter of common courtesy. Handle the homeless man on the streets with the same dignity and respect as you would the President of The United States.

Be honest *now*, and people will always respect you *later*! If a man shows interest in you and you tell him "I'm in a relationship" or "I'm married", that's not the same as saying "No, thank you. I'm not interested". Your relationship status can change any day, and by using that as a scapegoat, you are giving him *hope* for the future! And with hope... you can rest assured that you will continue to hear from this guy, see this guy, and he will constantly inquire about your current relationship status in hopes that he can somehow find a place in your life.

Relationships aren't for everybody; Relationships are for the "ready"! With this in mind, you are not obligated to "play ball" each and every time a man shows interest in you. What you can do is, offer an opportunity for you to talk more and get to know each other better as friends. Friendship is the key to having a longer lasting relationship. If you can start there, you both will have the opportunity to see the value in being a part of each other's lives, or the lack thereof. By denying a person this access, you cut off the possibilities to find romance, to network, and to build a new friendship. When meeting new people, you don't lose anything, but there's no limit to what you could gain if you take the time to figure out what value this person can add to your life.

Your personal contact information (i.e. your email address, phone number, Facebook, Twitter, other social networks) is just that… "Personal". This information should only be given to the men you would possibly like to have a personal relationship with. If you're in business, give only your business contact info to eliminate any and all ambiguity. Once you give a man your personal contact info, you are giving him hope, so choose wisely who you would like to give this hope to, and refrain from giving this access to men you never want to see or hear from again.

The introduction is everything! If a man approaches you with dignity and respect, then he may be someone worth keeping in touch with. There is power in networking! Your network should be filled with people who have an interest in you and/or your endeavors! The challenge for you should be to get your admirers to show interest in your life, business, events, projects, etc.

Try getting him to become a loyal *supporter*, and you'll have an idea of how loyal a *person* he can be. If he passes the test, keep him in mind for possibly a better position in your life. If he fails, keep him exactly where he currently is! By rejecting a man, you eliminate any and all possibilities for growth! His moral will be so beaten down that the initial interest he had in you will be gone… and replaced with slight resentment! A man who resents you is less likely to support your interests, your ideas, your business, or be there for you in your time of need.

Life is about building relationships and leaving

behind legacies! Rejecting men won't add value to your life or his. Instead of rejecting the men who show interest in you, respectfully decline his advances/proposals while still being open to a professional or platonic friendship. If the presentation/introduction is anything less than respectable, by all means, close the door. For everyone else, leave the door cracked!

A Lady Waits For A Gentleman

It's always fun to be adventurous and try new things; however there are certain roles that a man and a woman should play when it comes to dating and relationships. Times have changed, but principles have not! It's customary for a man to take the initiative and let a woman know that he's interested in pursuing her; this establishes him as a man who knows how to take control. One of the perks of being a woman is that men love doing nice things to win your affection, so sit back, relax, and enjoy being a woman!

If a man is interested in you, he knows exactly where to find you, all he has to do is scope you out, determine whether it's safe to approach, and then make his move. After he approaches you, there's no question whether or not he's interested, so now it's simply a matter of you saying yes or no. There's more risk associated if you decide to take matters into your own hands, but since you're a woman, you don't have to take such risks. If you aren't sure how to attract a man simply by being "there", then perhaps this is a craft you should work on.

A woman should be able to attract a man simply by *being* a woman. A woman asking a man out on a date is risky business, and it has its pros and cons. A pro would be that a man will more than likely say "yes" if you asked him out on a date. A con would be that although he said "yes" and entertained you on a date, he will not value you enough to take you seriously long-term, no matter how well the date went. The reason for this is his motivation to take you out on a date was not inspired by his own genuine interest. In other words, "You were too easy".

46

When a man takes his own initiative to ask a woman out however, he's already established that he's interested and that you're worth spending time, energy, and money on. He also has a budget laid out just for your special outing together. If/when a woman asks a man out, she's putting him in a compromising position… sort of obligating him to spend time, energy, and money on her. A man wants to be in control or at least feel like he's in control at all times, so there's a reason why a man hasn't yet asked you out, or is reluctant to accept your invitation out. A man wants to be emotionally and financially stable before allowing a woman into his life, so if/when a man is finally ready to entertain a woman on the dating scene, it has to be on his terms.

A few more reasons why a man might not ask a woman out are:

*He's not emotionally available
*He's currently involved with someone
*He can't afford to take you out
*He doesn't feel you are worth taking out
*He's only interested in sex (with you)

When you allow a man to take the initiative and ask you out, you put yourself in a better position to measure his level of interest in you and test his character. When it's *his* idea, he will then feel obligated to plan the entire night out (i.e. researching and choosing a place for y'all to go based on everything you've told him about yourself). He'll be more than happy to spend money on your date because he'll choose a place that fits within his budget, and by showing this initiative, it becomes evident that he feels you're worth investing in, and that he values you for more than just sex. It would be in his best interest to be single if he's putting forth all this time, energy, and effort, otherwise once the truth comes to light, he'll have wasted his time, energy, effort, and money, not to mention he'll have lost your trust.

The purpose of dating is to have fun with individuals you might be potentially interested in growing with or that you're currently growing with. Although it may still be *fun* to go out on a date with a man you've just thrown yourself at, it probably won't bring you any closer to finding the man you'd be able to grow with due to the average male's psychological conditioning. A more effective approach would be to signal the guy you're interested in by giving him "The Look" and then allowing him to take full initiative. By taking this approach, you know whether or not he's interested in you. If he's not interested, he won't approach.

If he's shy and timid, he won't approach; if he's confident and has high esteem, he will approach. And that's the guy you want. Shy and timid won't come in handy later on down the line when you're faced with real life issues and you need a real man to step in and take charge, so don't pity him. After approaching you, exchanging info, etc. he will figure out what he needs to do next if he plans on seeing you again. In the mean time, sit back, relax and enjoy being a woman while he enjoys being a man. When it's your time to perform, show him your worth via conversation and interaction.

Find Your Own Man

There's an abundance of men in this world who selfishly pursue other women outside of their relationship and/or marriage. Sometimes they lie and lead a woman to believe they're single, but for the man who can't afford to have another woman text/call his phone, pop up at his job, or know where he lives, he has to be up front and honest about his current relationship status in order to potentially have an ongoing affair with the woman on the side while maintaining the relationship he has at home.

SIDE NOTE: When a person shows you who they are... believe them! This is one of the areas many women struggle with the most. A man will show a woman exactly who he is from the beginning, yet she expects him to be someone different in the end. Never allow yourself to get caught up with someone who's merely a convenience. Settle on the best possible option for you and your relationship's future.

For the cheating male, it's clear that he doesn't respect himself, his partner, his relationship, or the woman on the side if he's bold enough to proposition her for sex. He's in a state of immaturity that will continue until he's ready to grow up, or for as long as the women he encounters will allow him to. The woman he has at home offers him security; she's his safety net and he's not going to leave her for the woman on the side (unless he plans on using her as his next safety net). The woman he cheats with offers him adventure, and he doesn't look for anything more than adventure from these women. There's no hope for a future together, no marriage, no family, no happily ever after. Just a "good time"!

For him, this is all a game! He enjoys the thrill of living a double life and fooling everyone around him (even himself). His wake up call will come once he experiences heartbreak (i.e. His woman cheating on him). See Chapter 7 "Men can dish it, but can't take it…"As mentioned earlier, there are times where the guy might lead the girl on the side astray, assuring her that he's single just to get her into bed.

However, these truths are inevitably revealed long before sex ever occurs if you're taking the time to get to know each other properly. Not knowing whether or not a man is in a relationship or married insists that you haven't done your research and/or didn't start the relationship off with friendship as the foundation. When you do your research and start things off as friends, details of a person's character will begin to reveal themselves; intricate details that you may or may not like. You'll determine whether or not this person is deserving of more of your time, energy, and effort based on the things you've discovered in their personality & character.

SIDE NOTE: During the getting to know each other process, sex should be nowhere in the equation! You should be focused solely on getting better acquainted.

The women who knowingly entertain men who are in relationships are seduced by the thought of having a taste of something forbidden. She's intrigued by his personality and charisma, but totally ignores his *character*. She's aware that his heart belongs to another woman, and this is where the challenge lies. The girl on the side is envious of the relationship he has with his girlfriend/wife and she wants it for herself. She lacks romance in her life and at the same time, the cheating man longs to prove to someone *new* that he can offer such pleasures. They both temporarily meet one another's needs, so she's totally content with dealing with him no matter what his relationship status is because he makes her feel better about herself by offering a false sense of security.

In her heart, she knows it's all a lie, but she likes the way it makes her feel, even if only for a few hours. When she's with him, he makes her feel beautiful, desired, and appreciated. For those few hours they spend together, he makes her feel like no other man has made her feel before! The only problem is… these are things that he should be doing *exclusively* for *his* woman who he has at home. These are things that the woman on the side should be getting from the man she's in a loving, committed relationship with.

With that said, nothing serious should be expected from either party because they both are proving through their actions that they're disloyal and dishonest, and that's no way to start a healthy relationship. This is the equivalent of a boss evaluating an intern before deciding to give him/her a position. Based on your performance over a given trial period, you may or may not advance to the next level in the company. The same applies to relationships. Any person who exhibits poor character in the beginning of the relationship should not be given a higher position in your life.

Food, Sex & Peace of Mind

This relationship that the man and the girl on the side have together is a fantasy! Not real! A lie! The "joy" she feels from this man is nothing more than a performance that deserves an Oscar! Once he reaches his climax, he'll already be on his way down from his lustful high and right back to reality! The reality for *him* kicks in once he leaves her side and goes back to his real life at home. The reality for *her* kicks in right when he's gone and she's sitting at home all alone wondering when's the next time she'll be able to feel the way he made her feel again She's dependent on the love/comfort of another woman's man, instead of loving herself and sharing her love with a man of her own.

Better to have security within yourself, knowing that you are worth being treated like a Queen, with dignity, honor, and respect. Knowing that whomever you give your mind, body, and soul to should automatically reciprocate and make you feel special, make you feel loved, and make you feel appreciated. Be confident in knowing that there are an abundance of honorable, respectable, educated, career oriented men with values who will gladly give you their time, energy, and efforts, and make you feel good about yourself exclusively and you won't have to share him with anyone. If you're looking for love, hold up a mirror!

You have to love yourself before you can love someone else. Take as much time as you need to work on finding yourself, building up your confidence, self-esteem, and character so that the next man you give your mind, body, and soul to is someone who is truly deserving of this honor. Your body is a temple that should be guarded like heaven. Building an honest, loving relationship with someone takes work, and there's no easy way of getting it. When you put forth the effort to find love, you'll work that much harder to keep it.

Friends With Benefits

A man knows the role he wants for a woman to play in his life before he even meets her. Everything from the clothes you wear, to the place y'all meet, to the company you keep is a determining factor in which category a man will place you in. Once a man places you in that category, there's no getting out; his pride won't allow him to upgrade a woman who degraded herself from the beginning. When a relationship starts off with sex, a man conditions himself to treat a woman in the manner she treated herself (which in this case is like a piece of meat).

Since respecting you and treating you like a lady was never a requirement, he certainly won't *offer* you this special treatment. He instead will give you the indisputable title of a "Sex Slave". Relationships that start with friendship as the foundation have a better chance of survival beyond the bedroom walls. In fact, when a relationship starts off with sex, the man only wants to give that relationship *life* inside of the bedroom, and *death* everywhere else. For a man, the hopes of getting sex, is the driving force, which motivates him to be a gentleman.

Once he's got it, he can go back to being his true self again; which may very well include not being the friend you thought he was in the beginning. In his mind, your purpose in his life was to pleasure him sexually. If you're no longer available for that, the two of you have absolutely nothing to talk about (according to him). Anytime he reaches out to you, it will be to see if you're available for a sex session. Not to go out to dinner, not to see how you're doing, not just to hang out and have a good time. He'll be contacting you specifically for *sex*.

He might butter you up with some conversation, but at the end of that conversation, he'll be wondering when the next time you're coming over. This will remain true from now until the end of time (for him). It's always best to present yourself as the person you want to be known and remembered as. You don't get a second chance to make a first impression, so if you've tainted your image with one man, clean yourself up and try again with someone new; this time treat yourself with dignity and respect!

Once you've made a conscious decision to be a lady, be consistent with your character. There's no need to verbally announce your new lifestyle to anyone; people will inevitably see a change in you through your actions. If a man from your past contacts you to potentially behave in a way that's not in alignment with your character, use this as an opportunity to update him on the person you are *today*. In a very polite and very respectful manner, let him know that you are no longer interested in having sex with no strings and that you're interested in a committed relationship.

His reaction will be one of the following: 1) He will feel as though you're not worth giving that much time/energy/effort to and move onto the next (for now). 2) He will attempt to oblige and begin treating you like a lady. If he takes option 1, you'll see right away how little he values you, which in turn will help you to grow and will motivate you to never sell yourself short again. If he takes option #2, he will then have to prove himself by properly getting to know you, courting, spending time, and doing all of these things simply out of the goodness of his heart and with no *immediate* sex as a motivation. In many cases, since he knows in his heart that he doesn't truly respect you, this attempt will be very short lived and he will eventually cancel himself out. #WinWin

The most important thing to do is learn from your mistakes. None of the men you've had a friendship with benefits with will respect you (as a lady)... because respect was never a requirement in the relationship y'all had. Men will respect you when *you* respect yourself! We all reserve the right to be selective, so no matter who respects you and who doesn't, you should always count on respecting yourself. Because of this "stamp" you've placed on your life, anytime these men from your past see you, they will be reminded of all the good sex y'all used to have (above anything else). If he has your number, he might call, if he's on your FB, he might send you a message, and if he knows where you work, he might stop by. There's nothing you can do to turn that switch off for him.

His desire to have sex with you will be fresh and new each time he sees you, anytime he thinks of you, whenever he gets horny, whenever it's late and he's out of options, etc. You are labeled as a *convenience* for Life! *This* is what comes with that territory. But that doesn't mean you have to stop living your life. Be genuine and sincere when you say you want to change, and continue to carry yourself with dignity and respect. The new men that come into your life will see you for the person that you are, and he will have to make a choice whether or not he's willing to deal with a woman who has a promiscuous past.

As long as you leave the men from your past in

the past, you can focus more on "you" in your present and your future. Continue to work on yourself, and present yourself in the way that you want to be perceived. You won't be able to change the way the men from your past think of you, but you can certainly reinvent yourself, and present your new image to the new men that you meet. The key is being true to yourself, being consistent, and making sure that you *stay* on this honorable path.

Chapter Three

Date with a Purpose

The Sole Purpose of Dating

Being single has its perks! You get to come and go as you please, you don't have to answer to anyone, there are no set rules that you have to abide by... and you feel as though you have total *freedom*! This is great until you want *romance* in your life. Sure, there are people you can call on to have a drink with, hang out with, or even sleep with from time to time, but that's only if/when *they're* available. The lack of consistency in your love life is one of the biggest drawbacks of being single. In order to gain consistency and longevity in your love life with someone of substance, you may be required to commit yourself to being with that person, and one of the best ways to figure out who will fit that mold is by getting to know new people (i.e. dating).

Now before you can even think about going on a date, you first have to look yourself in the mirror and evaluate the person that you are (inside and out). When you look in the mirror, you have to believe in your heart that you are a worthy candidate for dating, and then you have to actually possess qualities and characteristics that prove to your admirers that you are a worthy candidate. If you're evaluating yourself and *you* don't feel as though you're worthy, it's possible that the eligible bachelors that you meet will feel the exact same way. So be sure that you're *ready* to start dating before you actually get out there on the dating scene.

Now that you've evaluated yourself, your esteem is high, confidence is through the roof, you look good/smell good/feel good, you're independent, educated, you have your own money, you live on your own, etc. it's time to open yourself up to the possibility of entertaining men who mirror everything that you are

60

or reflect who you aspire to be. This means that the person you entertain should also have high esteem, confidence through the roof, looks good/smells good/feels good, is independent, educated, has their own money, is living on their own, etc. Just like you! *This* should be a bare minimal requirement! Remember the evaluation you did before you left your house. Know your worth and don't settle for anything less!

Side note: Finding your match isn't about *money*; it's about morals, values, character, personality, and sharing common interests.

Men are hunters and they like a challenge, so there will always be men who are ready/willing/available to date you *if* he feels you are worthy, and can sense that *you* feel you are worthy. You should use dating as a way to get closer to someone you are already in a relationship with or someone you see as a potential candidate for marriage; not everyone gets a date! You will find though, that not every man you see as potential will be a good fit, but it's an experience nonetheless. And since you can't predict how each date will turn out, don't put all your eggs in one basket. Line up multiple dates with different men (as they come) just to keep your options open.

After you've made a connection with one of the men you're dating, continue to strengthen your bond through steady conversation and interaction. Once you're comfortable and feel he's earned the privilege of getting a title, prepare yourself to be asked for exclusivity and begin to grow *together*. It is at this point you no longer have to worry about where your hugs and kisses are going to come from, and you can feel confident in knowing that your new partner will be more than happy to deliver his time, energy, and plenty of love whenever you call. You now have *exclusivity*! And being exclusive with someone is a wonderful feeling!

Dating isn't just for single folks; it's a way to have fun with a potential partner *and/or* your actual partner. One common mistake that many people in relationships make is that they stop competing for their significant other's love and affection. The competition never stops competing, so neither should you or your man! If you're in a relationship or marriage, *dating* should be a highlight in the relationship; something to look forward to. Keep the fun and excitement flourishing throughout your relationship; it doesn't have to be expensive, but make it a night to remember.

Get Back On The Dating Scene

Men look for women to get closer to on a daily basis. If you're interested in dating, being in a relationship, marriage, having a family etc., you have to start from the very beginning like any other major project in life. It can be a slow process at times, but it's well worth the wait! The first step has nothing to do with *him* and everything to do with *you*; that step is… making yourself "date worthy". A man can sense when a woman has no confidence, low self-esteem, doesn't know her worth, or simply doesn't match the criteria for what he looks for in a woman, so don't worry about doing anything special to attract a man; all you have to do is to continue to focus on being the best person you can be!

Your worth is determined by the value you add to the lives of *others*. That means for example, if a man is looking for a woman who can cook, you'll be a worthy candidate for *him* if you know how to cook. If you don't know how to cook, he may still see value in you as a person, however there's a slight chance that you might not be his ideal candidate for a wife. In the event a man does not want to proceed with a date, don't beat yourself up about it, just get back to *you* and wait for the *next* candidate to come along. There are millions of men in the world and you only need *one*.

When it comes to dating, a man likes the idea of being the pursuant; this allows him the time to budget, plan, and decide exactly *which* lady he would like to invest his time, energy, and money in. Before a man will consider dating a woman, he wants to be financially stable so that he can show you a nice time, and be emotionally available so that he can be open to receiving you. For these reasons alone, a man does not like to be prompted for a date; he will pursue dating when *he* is ready. If a man is financially stable, is emotionally available, and is genuinely interested in pursuing a relationship with you, he will be more than happy to offer to take you out on a date.

In the meantime, don't sit around waiting for some guy to call and ask you out! If you're that anxious to go out on a date, date yourself! Yes, date yourself! Get to know yourself a bit better and get comfortable doing fun and invigorating things on your own. Be independent until interdependence is required. If you don't want to be alone, call up a friend or a family member and enjoy the company of people you know and love minus the pressure of any sexual advances.

Treating *yourself* can also help you develop the standard for which you like to be treated. When a man finally does ask you out on a date, you can use your experience dating *yourself* to measure whether he will be a liability or an asset to your life. Taking yourself out will also give you an idea of what it's like for a man to pay for himself *and* for you on a date. Since dating can get quite expensive, it's a good idea to be flexible on the creative ideas he comes up with to be in your company, and by all means show appreciation. A lot of women find themselves in relationship trouble because they lack patience and get stuck with the wrong man.

Being *single* doesn't mean you have to be *lonely*; there are many ways to occupy yourself and your time to avoid settling for just *any* man. Stay focused on your health, education, career, and future; focus on a man only when he focuses on you. You can rush a man into bed, but you can't rush him into a date, a relationship, or a marriage. Let the man who is *ready* to start dating come looking for *you*.

Men who are not financially or emotionally stable won't opt to get financially or emotionally involved with a *new* woman. In other words, his only interest will be going *to* the bedroom and *out* the door with you. He already has it programmed in his mind that he can't afford to date you, or he's still emotionally attached elsewhere, and the only investment he is able/willing to make is with his penis. As a woman who has high standards and is looking for more substance, bypass these types of men as they will prove (over time) to be spiritually, emotionally, financially, and even physically draining. We're moving forward, not backwards, so only entertain those who have worth and know yours.

When it comes to dating, a man will put forth time, energy and effort *because* she is the one, not to figure out if she's the one. Do not be offended if a man you have great conversations with, and appear to have a great connection with, doesn't look to proceed towards dating with you. A man knows in his heart when he's found a good woman, however if he's going to share his world with a woman for *life*, he's looking to invest in a *great* woman. Don't allow a man's lack of interest in pursuing you to discourage you; continue to work on being the best woman you can be, and you'll continue to attract quality men who see value in you.

Keep your options open! Since pursuing a man on your own accord is a definite way to scare men away, enjoy the eligible bachelors who seek your hand. You've got a life, you've got work, and then you've got leisure; you'll be so busy with life that the men you come across will have to get in where they fit in or get lost. They will sense that you're busy and want to take full advantage of the time that you *do* have available for them. Once you've exchanged numbers, wait patiently for him to be the aggressor and contact you. Once he calls you, make the best of the conversation by telling him details about yourself. Tell him about your education, career, spiritual beliefs, relationship with your family, favorite food/drinks, likes/dislikes, the kind of sports you like to watch, favorite movies, favorite books, and more!

When you give a man details about your life, he'll have enough information about you to plan a date that caters to your taste. Feel free to let him know where your favorite restaurant is, but don't make it a requirement that he takes you there on the first date. Since it's highly improbable that you'll be paying for the date, allow him the opportunity to research places that work within his budget. Also, when you're getting to know a potential romantic interest, be sure not to come off primarily as a "cool chick" or a "home girl". A man wants a woman who's going to be a *woman*. He's got enough "homies"… And so do you!

On date night, do your hair/make-up, and wear something that's flirty and fun! Avoid anything "slutty" because then he'll just want to "bed you" right then and there and you'll never get those lustful thoughts out of his head… *EVER*! No matter how hard you try! If the date goes well, you should (again) be *patient* and wait for him to reach out to you and ask for another date. To avoid being overly anxious, keep yourself busy with work/life and perhaps entertaining other admirers who are interested in growing with you. Don't concern yourself with how others view you for dating multiple people at once; you don't know what's going on in that *one* date's life, nor do you have any control over him.

He could be in a relationship, he could only be after sex, he could *not* be that into you, or whatever! But you don't want to find yourself being too anxious over this one "great" date you had. And you *will* feel as though most of your dates went fairly well considering you haven't been on the dating scene in a while. So again I stress… be patient!

Now if you like the guy that you're dating, show him a little love and let him know you are in fact enjoying his company. You don't want to be cold and not give him any signals at all. You have to remember… *he* is dating multiple women too! And he can't afford to invest his time, energy, and money on a woman who's not giving him any feedback on how the date is going or how you feel about him. In order to get a 2nd date from him, he has to feel the connection/feel the vibes/feel the energy and know that you're into him. While you're dating these multiple men, evaluate them based on their character (i.e. his actions).

Is he opening doors for you? Is he making arrangements and paying for the date? Was he on time? Was he a gentleman? Some men don't *know* better, while others simply don't *do* better. Either way, you will have your answers on or before the first date. It's up to *you* to know your worth and not settle for anything less than what you feel you deserve.

After dating a guy, talking to him, getting to know him, etc., consider giving him a promotion if you are satisfied with his performance. By now, he will want to have more of your time, and he will without a doubt want to sleep with you. If you give him sex before a commitment, you run the risk of him no longer wanting to compete for your time. There's no need to give him an ultimatum as far as committing to you, because by now, *he* will want to make progress with you after waiting it out for all this time. Allow *him* to be the aggressor and ask *you* if you'd like to become exclusive.

Between your work schedules, your daily life, dating other guys, etc., he'll want to secure a place in your life that will guarantee him more exclusive time with you. After all the time/energy/effort/money he's been investing in you, he will want to know where things are going. Or better yet, he'll be wondering *if* things *can* go somewhere… because you're beginning to get *expensive* lol. If a man willingly invests his time/energy/effort/money into you that is a great sign that he's genuinely interested. Time, energy, effort, and money mean a lot to a man. So if he's putting forth this type of effort, you either reward him because you want it to continue, or you leave him alone because you're not interested.

Once you feel you're ready, put yourself out there, get some dates lined up, and enjoy yourself. Your first date is more than just a good time, it's an interview, so be sure to be super observant and make mental notes of his behavior. After a date, make a decision whether or not you'd like to get closer to him, and work towards that goal. Always be considerate of other people's time and money; if you're not genuinely interested in a man, have some integrity and gracefully decline his offer. Happy dating!

Ways of Knowing A 1st Date Went Well

It's important to have a few conversations over the phone prior to going out on an actual date so that you can get a feel of one another's personality/character. This is also a great way to fill each other in on your personal interests, likes/dislikes, favorite foods/drinks, hobbies, education, work, background, spiritual beliefs, etc. This gives the man an opportunity to register everything that you've mentioned and figure out what would be best for a first date. By him doing this, it shows that he's willing to put forth effort into making sure that the first date isn't completely *generic* and that he feels you are worth going the extra mile for. This is a great way to start a relationship off, and this is the first sign to see just how interested he is in potentially building a long lasting relationship with you.

If you don't have the opportunity to date much, be sure to choose someone you actually want to spend time with when you do. A date is something fun to look forward to that will take you away from the stress in your everyday life, kids, job, and other responsibilities. You get to throw on something nice, relax, and see what lies ahead with an admirer. The less interested a man is in a woman, the more difficult it will be for him to bring himself to take initiative, plan a date, court a woman, and actually *pay* for the date because he knows that he's simply *not* that interested in her or he only wants to sleep with her. So if a man takes this step, it's at least a sign that he's willing to put forth some type of effort and see how things go.

There's no love lost when going out on date with someone you're curious about; just two adults out having a good time. Being on a date requires a person's full attention, face-to-face interaction, eye contact, intellect, and more importantly, it involves both of your time, energy, effort, and money. The first date sets the tone on whether or not there will be a 2nd date, or possibly a future, so anything that's in your control should be kept under control (i.e. Putting your cell phone on vibrate so that there are no interruptions, making sure not to look at other people whom you may find attractive as they walk by, and also eliminating any future obligations he may feel you owe him by offering to pick up your own tab). These are signs that you respect one another and want to maintain that respect for future encounters.

A date can either seem too long, or too short, but time flies when you're having fun. If the energy is great, the vibes are there, and the conversation is flowing, neither one of you will be paying attention to the time. In fact, I'd be willing to bet that if one of you had an important appointment scheduled immediately after the date, that you would be willing to run a few minutes late just to spend a little more time with one another. This is when you know things are going *really* well!

At the end of the date there will be a warm feeling in your heart and you'll want to somehow show your affection to this person. This is when you pull back a little so that the man will want to do something to *earn* those privileges in the future. Pull back *graciously* (not with an attitude); you don't want to confuse him and ruin your chances for a 2nd date. You also don't want to give him *too* much *too* soon; a simple hug and a kiss on the cheek will suffice. If you allow him to caress your body, French kiss you, or do anything that's too seductive, he'll want to skip the romantic process and head right to the bedroom. Don't be a tease. If you're going to be a lady, be consistent through and through.

If the date did not go well, you'll immediately notice a lack of interest in his eyes, in the tone of his voice, and in his body language during the date. He'll even sometimes portray a lack of respect by doing things such as looking at people whom he finds attractive walking by, texting, answering his phone, or he may even cut the date short due to an "emergency" or a "meeting". He might be bold enough to *request* that you go Dutch, or if he picks up the tab, he might do so with an attitude. He'll only make sure you made it home safely if he drove you there. If you hear from him again, it won't be to go on a 2nd date... it will be to come over to his place or to yours. This is how males handle a date that didn't go well.

Men don't write women off completely. When a man isn't interested in a woman, he'll still in fact sleep with her, but he will no longer consider her for a relationship or even a 2nd date for that matter. There's a world of possibilities as to what a person might do when they're simply not that into you. But what counts is the way you both feel about each other after this 1st encounter. If you don't sense an immediate desire to be connected during and after the date, chances are the chemistry between you and the other person isn't strong enough to warrant a 2nd date or further exploration. If this is the case, cut your losses, and devote your time/energy/effort/money into someone you can potentially grow with.

If the date went well, you will notice that he will

Food, Sex & Peace of Mind

continue to do things (after the date is over) to prove
that he is worthy of and interested in having more of
your time (i.e. Picking up the tab, opening doors,
making sure you made it home safely, and then... you
will hear from him *again* before he goes to bed letting
you know that he enjoyed his time with you). He will
reach out to you whenever you're on his mind
throughout the week, and he will inquire about when he
can see you again. If this is the case, you've got yourself
a winner. Have fun on your 2nd and future dates! Good
luck ;)

Single Parent Dating

If you are a single mother, your primary concern should be the well-being of your children, their upbringing, their support system, the influences coming in and out of their lives, etc. If/when you end the relationship with the child's father, you should be very careful with the next man/men you allow in your kids' lives because it will affect the way your child feels about you, and it will also affect your child's behavior in the future. When you're finally ready to get back on the dating scene, it's important that when you're getting to know a guy, you give pertinent details about your life (upfront) such as "I'm a single parent raising a child".

You should also be sure to get the man you're dating's feedback on how he feels about dating a single parent. While you're talking and getting to know one another, discuss relevant things, such as morals, values and life principles that you both live by. In these discussions, you should make it clear that you are interested in a commitment, that you respect your children, and will not entertain anything short of a relationship of substance that will lead to marriage. At these early stages, removing sex will allow you to measure his sincerity in making a decision on whether or not he feels you're worth investing more time/energy/effort/money in.

Side note: Do not assume just because he too has kids that he's willing to date, or is looking for a woman who also has kids. Ask questions, and test him to see where he stands.

Test the man you're dating's character every

chance you get! Ask him what his relationship is like with his mother, his ex-wife/girlfriend, and his own children. BTW the way he treats "you" is in no way shape or form an indication of how he will treat your child. You have to actually allow him to meet and interact with your children to see how far he is willing to go to gain your child's approval. If he doesn't go the distance to win your child over, then he should no longer be considered as a candidate for a relationship because your child is your heart… and your heart is what he's ultimately trying to win. And furthermore, if your child does not accept this man or doesn't approve of him, then you should respect your child's decision and choose your child over *him*.

Your child's approval is certainly needed before you decide to proceed with a new romantic relationship. Yes, we know that *you* are comfortable with this new guy, but your *kids* need to be comfortable with this new man who's coming into their family and spending time with their beloved mother. By no means should he be forced onto your kids simply because you're lonely and need a man. Forcing a new man on a child could cause resentment towards *him*, but more importantly towards *you*!

Your children are forever! A man can leave you and forget about you at any given time if he no longer wants to deal with the total package that comes along with being with you!!! If for whatever reason, he decides not to be a part of your life, you'll be left with the same group of people that you started with (your children). So be sure to make decisions that work best for the *family* and not just for *you*.

If you put *yourself* first, and allow yourself to

get close to a man, start sleeping with him, etc. before he wins your children's hearts, you'll be heading towards the point of no return! You'll want this man in your life so badly because of the way he makes *you* feel, that you totally forget about your heart... your world... which is your *child*. Meanwhile, your child gets stuck with the *leftovers*. Not to mention, there's a chance that this new guy will be so comfortable and used to being with just *you*, that once your kid comes into the picture, it will be a "buzz kill" for him. He might love *mommy*, and he might care about mommy... but that doesn't have anything at all to do with this kid you have hanging around the house.

You have to make having a relationship with your child a *requirement* for the new guy (in the beginning). Don't be afraid to lose him! If he doesn't want to have a relationship with your child... he shouldn't be rewarded with the privilege of being in a relationship with *you*! Unfortunately, there are too many women out there who are afraid that a man will run as soon as she makes "being a step-dad" a requirement to be with her. But talking about it is something that you will have to do if you want to become serious with a man and make him a part of your family.

You're not a single bachelorette anymore! You're a *package deal* now. This is your *new* life! The new guys that come along have no choice but to either accept this or explore other options. If he's looking to simply date and have sex, then he needs to find a woman who can afford to do so.

A single woman raising a child though needs to find a man who can and will be there for her *and* her child. In fact, his relationship with your child should be so strong that if the two of you break-up, he would still want to be involved in your child's life… and your child would still want to be involved in his life. This is the kind of man you need. But in order to figure out if he's that type of man, you have to put him through vigorous tests in the *beginning*!

Everything is always great in the beginning when it's just the two of you, but you also have to measure his level of interest and compatibility with your kid. Some of the signs to look for are: Is he genuine and sincere? Is he offering to do activities that are kid friendly? Is he interacting with your child? Is he taking a personal/genuine interest in them? Is he compassionate? Or is he solely interested in *you*? These are things you can see with your eyes, hear with your ears, and feel with your heart. If he fails this test in the beginning, he should no longer be considered for a relationship or marriage because your child comes first.

Now if you didn't put him through all of these tests and you let him slide, by sexing him, committing to him, moving in together, marrying him, etc., then you're setting yourself up to potentially get your heart broken. By this point, you'll have grown emotionally attached to him without him first winning your heart (which is your child), and now it's a gamble whether or not the love he has for *you* will trickle down to your kids. If at any point you realize that a man doesn't love your child the way a husband/father should (as if it were his own), you will *then* begin to realize just how much of a first priority your child's well being is to you. You're also going to recognize how little this man means to you in comparison to your child.

If his heart was not involved with your child from the beginning, you can't possibly expect for his heart to miraculously be involved later on simply because you're in a relationship or married. This is a sign that his interest was solely in *you!* Since bonding, loving, and respecting your children was never a prerequisite to being with, he'll be reluctant to honor these sudden requests later on in the relationship.

It's extremely important to know how the man you let into your life feels about your child before getting too involved with him. Who knows? He might think your kids are annoying, spoiled, have no discipline, aren't too bright, looks too geeky, talks too much, or whatever! The sky is the limit! If while dating a man, and after you've introduced him to your child, you notice that he's not eager to see your child again, doesn't talk about your child, or doesn't mention your child at all, then you should have a conversation with him about what he thinks about *your* child. Use this information to make your decision on whether you want to continue to deal with him or not.

You can test the waters by casually introducing your children to the man you're dating and get a feel of how they interact with one another. The clear cut signs will be there from the very beginning, and it will be indication of what you can look forward to in the end. This is your future we're talking about and not every man you meet will be worthy of being in your child's presence. This could mean being single for 5, 10, 15+ years! However long it takes! But your kids need to be loved, respected, and comfortable at all times, even if it makes you feel uncomfortable.

Online Dating

In this day and age, there are more and more people taking advantage of technology and applying it to their daily lives. We are no longer in the era of the telegram where our sources of communication were extremely limited. Social networking sites such as Facebook, Twitter, and various sites specifically designed for dating have made it easier for people to make a connection for whatever purposes one chooses (i.e. keeping in touch with friends, business, dating, etc.). There's really no such thing as "online dating". "Online" is simply the place where the introduction is made between two people.

Anywhere there are women, men will follow, and men will pursue them with the hopes of one day connecting on a romantic level. This is true for social networking sites, the grocery store, school, church, the library, you name it! Men are always on the lookout for women they can potentially get closer to *romantically*, and especially online. If you're interested in dating, relationships, or marriage, it's a great idea to keep an open mind to the possibility of meeting new people any and everywhere *people* can be found. Since the majority of people spend a fair amount of their time online, there's a high probability that men will approach you there. The possibilities of meeting someone new and making a love connection right from your computer are endless.

The beauty of meeting someone online is you have the opportunity to research any of your admirers *before* taking any action. Take Facebook for example, you can look through their pictures and get a feel of their personality and character, you can also see their

78

relationship status, what friends you have in common, location, education, career, and other pertinent information all before even saying hello. You'll notice that people on social networking sites always publicly reveal things about themselves; not realizing how much it reflects their character. You could probably learn more about a person's character in one minute by viewing their online profile than in one hour of talking to them in person.

Before a man introduces himself to a woman, he studies her momentarily, and then figures out exactly what he's going to say to try and convince her that he's someone worth knowing. A woman won't admit it, but she prefers being seduced over hearing the absolute honest truth. A man would love to walk right up to a woman and say "Hey, let's have sex right now!", but that doesn't work well with women. He instead has to be gentle, use a subtle approach, and somehow convince her that he's after more than just her body. Since you've never met this man and you haven't had the opportunity to fully assess him, your mood, combined with the words that come out of his mouth, matched with his approach will be the determining factor in whether or not you entertain him.

Never listen to a man's words… always follow his actions. When you follow a man's actions, you will see for yourself what he values, how he carries himself, and how he treats other people. When you listen to a man's words, he'll tell you any and everything you want to hear. Thanks to the power of the Internet, you can follow a man's *actions* without him even uttering a single word. Since getting to know a man's character has been made so readily available via his online profile, use this information to your advantage. If you're a beautiful woman, you're going to constantly get propositioned for dates on and offline, so instead of closing off the possibility of meeting men online, simply do your "research" and be selective.

When you meet someone on the Internet, there's no obligation to actually pursue one another, it's simply an exchange of words amongst two online friends. You'll come to find through your conversations and interactions that there are *many* interesting people right there in your social network that could potentially add value to your life on some kind of level. If they were good enough to be added to your network, they should at least be good enough to entertain in conversation. You don't have to date any and every person who shows interest in you, but there's no harm in entertaining the men who *do* show interest in you. With any and everything you do in life, you want to go where you're celebrated, not tolerated, so feel free to give those men on your friend list a chance if they prove to be worth it!

If you're uncomfortable exchanging contact info, you can take advantage of private messaging or instant messaging and get better acquainted right in the comfort of your own home. You don't lose anything from building relationships with new people; however you could potentially gain a new lover, friend, or even a business partner. You might have a business idea that you're trying to get off the ground and you need more supporters; what better people to market to than the men right there in your network who show interest in you? This could possibly give them the opportunity to take a genuine interest in your life and you in theirs.

#WinWin

No matter where you meet a person, "dating" is something that has to take place in person. When you meet them online, you're simply granted the opportunity to pre-evaluate them before taking the extra step of meeting them in person. A first date should always be in a public setting simply for your safety and comfort; don't let *fear* be an obstacle that you place before you and an admirer. Let go of your fear, and enjoy the people who take an interest in your life no matter where you meet them.

Keep in mind that a man who's viewing your online profile also has access to your profile pictures, status updates, etc. and will very well make a judgment of your character before he approaches you. Men are very visual, so always present yourself in the way you want to be perceived. If for example you're half naked in your profile picture, you're going to attract men who are interested in your body as opposed to your heart and mind. They probably won't even bother reading your profile because they've already made the determination that the bedroom is the only place they're willing to go with you. Your image reflects who you are as an individual, so don't think that because it's "Just Facebook" that you'll be given a pass for acting out of character.

If you carry yourself with dignity and respect at all times, the men you attract will do the same. There are plenty of available options that men can choose from online, so make sure you're attracting these admirers for the right reasons. Relationships are about two individuals coming together to become *one*! If you're going to date, pursue a relationship, or pursue a marriage, it's going to require you to be vulnerable and trust your partner. Sure you could get your heart broken, sure you could get abandoned, and sure you could be disappointed, but part of the beauty of being in love is enjoying what's presently happening and not knowing what the future holds.

If you meet someone and there's chemistry, don't hesitate to act on those feelings and take a chance on love. Not everything in life will be logical or practical; some things are done simply out of love because love has no reason! Life is short, and you don't have to live your life in fear, or have regrets about things that you should've, could've, or would've done. Don't let work and school be the only things in life that you go hard for; *people* are also worth it!

There's a world of educated, career driven, quality men of substance online, and nowadays you can even search them by *key words*. Use this to your advantage and explore the possibilities of love! Create a profile on a social network showing the world who you are, post a stellar profile picture and bio, and get ready for the quality men of substance to pour in. Happy Dating!

Date Multiple Men At Once

It's always a good idea to keep your options open when dating, because you never know what to expect out of guy. The last thing you want to do is waste your good years sitting around waiting on this *one* great guy you're dating to make things official. It's indeed honorable and respectable to be exclusive with one man, but only when that one man is exclusive with you! Be loyal only to those who are loyal to you.

If you're single and interested in being entertained by the opposite sex, take advantage of the wonderful world of dating. Dating is a great way to take your mind off of your regular, everyday life and have fun with someone you're mutually interested in. There's no obligation when dating someone, so you don't have to feel guilty about exploring multiple options. Just be sure not to take on so many options that you're unable to make a decision on who works best for your life. Date with a purpose! If the man you're considering dating isn't someone you see as potential, then focus more of your time on the candidates you *do* see as potential.

Spreading yourself *too* thin can possibly cause you to overlook a potentially great guy, so be sure to know how many you can handle at one time. Once you start to get closer to someone you like, it's ok to let go of the less qualified admirers and focus more of your time on the leading man. Between work, your regular everyday life, and dating multiple men, your time and energy will become quite limited. You want to leave room to develop genuine feelings for these men you're dating, so that hopefully in the near future things can develop into something more. On the plus side, being completely booked will make it easier for you to decline any men who are not worthy of your time. A great way to avoid being around the bad guys, is to surround yourself with the good guys.

A lot of women become "slaves" to the one man she's dating because she's allowing him to be her "only hope". Dating multiple men will prevent you all from falling victim to this vicious cycle. The great thing about dating is... there's no obligation! You're not required to sleep with any of these men, you don't have to promise them anything, and there's no commitment. But do note that the men who are showing interest in you are doing so as an *investment.* If you're not interested in at least exploring the possibility of getting closer to someone, save the man and yourself some time and decline the offers.

If you *are* interested in exploring new possibilities with these men, by all means enjoy the experience, and be selective. Not everyone gets a date! The men who are seeking your hand will see that you are busy with work, life, and other things, so they will try even harder to get your attention. You'll notice that some of the less patient and less interested men will sometimes kick *themselves* to the curb... because they don't see the value in investing in you, can't afford to invest in you, or never even planned on investing in you. This is how you weed out the serious men from the ones who only want to get close to your body. A great way to measure a man's interest in you is by the amount of time, energy, effort, and money he invests in you.

Time and money are two things that men value and don't easily part with. When you're single, work on being the best person you can be so that you can attract the best people. A man wants a woman while she's at her best, and avoids women who are at their worst. People invest *more* if what they're investing in is in high demand and/or prove to be of great value. If a man is at a point in his life where he's achieving great things, he's also going to want to associate with a woman who is doing the same and can potentially upgrade him.

When you're single, you are free to do whatever it is you want and you won't have to answer to anyone but yourself; that's the beauty of being independent. No matter how long you've been dating someone, if the two of you are not *exclusive*, you're not obligated to inform a man on who you're talking to/dating/sleeping with/etc. until the two of you have become exclusive. A confident man of substance will either use this insight as motivation to gain exclusivity from you, or move along to someone else whom he feels will be more worthwhile. Don't worry, this is simply a matter of pride and ego; you can stroke his pride and ego, once he's become *the* man in your life, not *a* man in your life.

While you're single... enjoy mingling! Men totally understand that if he doesn't ask you to be his woman, then you have the right to entertain anyone you please. If he asks, you can tell him, "I'm exploring my options". There are some men who won't be too happy about this practice, but they have no choice but to respect it. Truth be told, the only reason why he's not too thrilled about it is because he's no longer in a position of *power*.

To be in power means to be able to influence or

be in control. The only way a man should be allowed to influence your life is when he is committed to being influential in your life. Single bachelors have been playing the "date multiple women at once" game for ages! He dates multiple women at once so that he can maintain his regular dosage of sex, while also maintaining his independence. A man already knows the role he wants for a woman to play in his life before he even meets her, so if he doesn't see potential in a woman upfront, he'll *still* date her simply to keep her entertained and keep the sex coming.

This is why it's important that *you* should also date multiple people because there are many men out there who are simply not interested in settling down, but will still go through the motions! Some guys are "dating pros" and offer a false sense of security because he knows just what to do, what to say, and how to make a woman feel good. After a great evening though, the man might disappear off the face of the earth, and totally confuse you as to *what just happened.* You might think he's not interested, or he's busy, and both could very well be the case, but one of the most relevant reasons of all is that he's simply entertaining *other* women. A man doesn't abandon a woman that he plans on taking seriously; he instead will focus his time, energy, and effort on that one woman *if* he's ready.

If he's not ready, he will keep her as a convenience and reach out to her when it's convenient. If you allow a man to get too close too soon, he may feel a sense of entitlement. As a single woman, you have to stand firm, and make it clear to a man that you are not *his* woman, and that you're merely a woman he's dating. If his pride and ego can't handle the fact that you have an actual *right* to date other men and figure out what's best for you, then by all means... *he* has the right to remove himself from your life all together. If he decides to leave, make a note of his lack of loyalty and willingness to fight for you. When a person shows you who they are in the beginning, you can't expect them to be any different in the end.

If you're living your life, you're not worried about what somebody else is doing; if you're worried about what somebody else is doing, you're not living your life. You can't control what other people do with their lives, you can only control *you*! This holds true no matter what type of relationship you have, but with a commitment comes *trust.* Before a commitment is in place, you have to be realistic with yourself and *expect* that the other person you're dating is living their lives and doing whatever it is they want to do. This is why it's important to date with a *purpose* and give more of your time to individuals who prove to be interested in a relationship that holds value.

Often times when you only have *one* option, you'll find yourself clinging, and that's never an admirable trait that men look for in a woman. Sure... the idea of having you chasing behind him might work well for him when he's bored, but when you're dependent on a man who's not *your* man, the sense of obligation he feels will become a turn off! A man likes to have a woman who has other options, but chooses *him* as her option. He likes the fact that she's in high demand, has limited time to spare, but out of all the admirers, she finds joy in spending her time with *him*.

By the way ladies, the idea of a woman dating multiple men isn't to *use* them. The idea behind a woman dating multiple men is a strategy to find a worthy suitor to be in a relationship with. This method is designed to help you avoid getting stuck dating the guys who aren't serious, and connect you with the ones who are. Now that you're back on the dating scene, it's time that you look out for *your* best interest.

Dating should be a mutually beneficial arrangement, so be sure that what you're putting into the date is something that *he* will value. The both of you are investing your time and energy, however if you've dating for a while, it's highly probable that he'll be investing his money into you. Be creative and come up with different ways you can add value to his life so that he can continue to be motivated to do nice things for you.

Chapter Four

Relationships Aren't For Everybody

Relationships Are Only For The "Ready"

From the moment we take our first breath, we are born into a relationship. We are in a committed relationship with our parents and/or caregivers for 18 years, and throughout those 18 years we are given instructions on how to live our lives, what's best for us, what's not, etc. We are dependent on the love, money, and resources that are being provided by the people who run the homes that we live in. For 18 years, we behave in a way that's pleasing to the eyes of our parents, so that we can remain in their favor; and when they're not looking, we do what's best for *us* in the shadows.

Anytime one relationship ends, there should be a healing process to help you gather yourself financially, spiritually, physically, and emotionally. There's no time limit on how long this process should take, but the purpose is to establish independence! Take the lessons you've learned from your relationship with your parents and use them to plan for a better future (on your own). This journey will allow you to see your strengths, weaknesses, and will help you appreciate the value you add to your own life, which is a reflection of the value you can add to the lives of others.

There comes a time in every young adult's life where he/she has to leave the nest and spread their wings independently. Being able to stand up on your own two feet shows that you are ready, willing, and able to be independent; Gaining independence is the first step towards becoming interdependent. When you work on being the best person that you can be, you'll attract the best people. Being single and independent grants you the time you need to focus on your heart, mind, body, and spirit! Taking time away from

90

relationships and focusing on *self*, just might be the answer to many women's relationship problems!

Being in a relationship with someone romantically is similar to a relationship with your parents. In order for any relationship to stay happy and healthy, there has to be rules, guidelines, and expectations that everyone is required to live up to. One of the main differences between a parent/child relationship and a boyfriend/girlfriend relationship though is that you get to *choose* who/when you want to be in a committed relationship with (based solely on *your* desire to be committed). If you don't have the desire to be in a committed relationship, spare yourself and simply enjoy living the single life. Being single is the thing you do when you're establishing/finding yourself and/or when you haven't met someone who meets your standards.

One of the keys to being in a happy/healthy relationship is being honest with yourself. Incorporate The 7 Habits of Highly Effective Relationships (According to Chey B.) These habits are Respect, Love, Honesty, Loyalty, Trust, Support, and Communication. If you don't have these very basic/mandatory qualities in your relationship, your relationship will not reach its fullest potential. Take as much time as you need to work on your heart, mind, body, and spirit, and to better prepare yourself to share your world with another person. If you're not ready, willing, and able to share your world, being single is probably the best way to go.

If you're going to be single… be single *by design* as opposed to being single *by chance*. Being single by *design* means that you're on a spiritual journey, and your goal is to find yourself and become a better you! Finding yourself means that you're not out looking for others; it's all about "you"! Single by *chance* means that you *were* on a journey and in love with someone, and then over time, love was lost. If love and happiness can be found inside of you, you'll never go a day without it. When you meet someone new, let them be an *addition* to the love and happiness you already have; this way if they ever leave or forsake you, you'll be happy and in love with or without them.

It's counter-productive to live a double life in secret; meanwhile you're telling your partner that you're committed to only them. You'll have more peace of mind being single and honest with yourself than you will with lying to your significant other. If you want your partner to stay, give them hope! If you want your partner to leave, give them doubt! When you finally decide to commit to someone, make sure that you are ready, willing, and able to be faithful, and that you have a genuine interest in contributing to their life.

There will be plenty of time to dedicate your life to someone, bare children, get married, and live happily ever after, but before you do that, enjoy being in a relationship with yourself. Being in a relationship with yourself will help raise your standards and help you to eliminate those who don't meet them. When your level of love, finance, spirituality, health, etc. is at an all-time high, you will *then* have the leverage to be matched with a suitable partner. You are who you attract, so work on being your best!

Being single allows you the time, space, and opportunity to do what's best for you, so take the time that you're by yourself to do just that! Go to school, establish a career, save up money, travel the world, meet/explore new people, and live life to the fullest (with no regrets). Do this until your heart is content and until you are ready for something *more*. When you're finished achieving your short-term goals and you're ready to pursue a long-term achievement with another person, seek someone who mirrors the person that you are or everything you aspire to be.

After you've done everything your heart desired as a single individual, settling with someone who's a good match will only upgrade your life. All of the wonderful things you've experienced *independently* can now be experienced *interdependently* if that's what you would like in a partner. Being in a relationship isn't an indication of your life ending; it's an indication of a new life beginning. Life is about building relationships and leaving behind legacies; we live in a world filled with people, no one is meant to live this life alone! Never look for a relationship, but always prepare your heart, mind, body, and spirit to be ready for one!

Long Distance Relationships

Let's be honest... You meet people where you meet people, and you fall in love with who you fall in love with. The person you fall in with could live anywhere on the planet and wherever *they* are... that's where *your* heart is. No matter where this man goes, you want to stay connected because he has a special place in your heart and you don't want to let it go. Sure you're not able to hug, kiss, touch, and engage in sexual activity, but those things aren't the driving forces behind your love for this person. You love this person because of the way they made you feel *inside*. No matter their distance away from you, you still have that special *feeling*.

The *option* of living within driving distance of the person you love isn't always an option. No matter where you meet a person though, it's important that you get to know them (inside and out) and start your relationship off as *friends*. When you start your relationship off as friends, you allow enough space and opportunity for things to grow *organically* and without any pressure. Leading solely with your emotions can set you up for heartbreak. Before you get yourself too emotionally attached, get to know who they are and get a better understanding of their position in life.

No matter whether you live right next door or thousands of miles away from one another, you can *still* bring joy to one another's lives, and if the two of you are determined to stay committed to a long distance relationship, there *is* hope for you both. It's important though to be honest with yourself and with your partner from the beginning. If you know in your heart that the distance between you two will be too much of a challenge, it's better to salvage the friendship that you have, than to commit to a relationship that you won't be able to stay fully committed to.

Weigh out the pros and the cons before making it official, and then do what's best for you. While committing to a long distance relationship may provide a sense of comfort in knowing that you "have somebody", you also have to consider the challenges that come with not being able to enjoy your partner physically. Relationships are designed to be spent *together*. Long distance relationships can keep you from not only seeing your partner, but it also prevents you from enjoying the admirers who are in close proximity who may also be interested in you.

There are some things that can be done from afar that can help keep the excitement going (i.e. phone conversations, texting, emailing, and even webcam). These methods are great, but you're eventually going to need face-to-face interactions to balance things out. Visiting one another at least once per month can help remove some of the tension and anxiety, but this all depends on the individual(s). You have to know your partner, and you have to know whether or not they are mature enough to handle these challenges and get through them *with* you.

When it comes to men and relationships, one of the main reasons why men commit is because they no longer have to worry about where their regular dosage of sex is coming from. If his significant other is in another state… he then has to worry about where his regular dosage of sex is coming from. Depending on the individual, this *could* cause a problem; so again, know the type of man you're dealing with. A man who has options will in fact explore his options if *you* are not an option.

Hope and *faith* is the driving force between making a long distance relationship work, but don't live on hope and faith alone. Be honest with yourself and with your partner, and don't be afraid to let go if staying loyal proves to be too much of a challenge. There a millions of men in this world and you only need "one". If you're looking to have a happy, healthy relationship with someone, seek someone who lives in close proximity to you so that you have a better chance at love.

A person who lives within driving distance from you can provide you with the love, affection, and regular dose of attention that you would want and need. We are all human and we long to share our worlds with another person, become closer with them, grow with them, and build a future with them. Put yourself in the best position to give love and receive love by finding someone within your reach who is ready, willing, and able to appreciate and reciprocate it.

Build A Relationship of Substance

Anytime you have the desire to enter into a relationship with someone, you should begin with the end in mind. Success is measured by one's ability to reach his/her goals, so if you want your relationship to be successful, set goals for yourself and work towards achieving them. Different people value different things, and this is especially true when it comes to the opposite sex. Some people value sex with no strings, some value monogamy, and some simply value no sex at all. Since values differ from person to person, it's important to discuss morals, values, and principles with the person you're getting to know long before getting emotionally and sexually involved. Sharing morals, values, and principles is a great way to start off any relationship, and it will help you attract the men you need, and avoid the men you don't.

Sex is great, and it plays a huge factor in any romantic relationship, however… all relationships and all *things* have to be built on a solid foundation… otherwise, it will eventually crumble. The foundation that makes a romantic relationship last longer is best known as *friendship*. Friendship is the *key* to romance! Through friendship, you will discover a great deal of pertinent information about a person's character that will help guide you towards deciding whether or not this person is right for you. Most men won't have the patience to wait 90 days (as Steve Harvey mentioned) for sex, but these are the types of men you want to avoid. 90 days isn't a deadline for sex, but more so a probationary period that allows you to feel him out.

Within a 90 day period, continue to live your life as you normally would, which will give you both the space and opportunity to miss one another. When you can find the time, talk to one another over the phone and share details of each other's lives; this will give you a list of great topics to spin off of on date nights. While getting better acquainted over the phone, you may even come to find that you're not interested in pursuing anything further than platonic friendship, and opt not to go out on a date. If you find this person to be interesting and if he possesses the moral fiber you look for in a man, by all means, give it a try. The goal here is to establish a foundation that you can fall back on for those times when you're not in the mood to do anything more than simply be in each other's company.

It's quite difficult to have dinner, cuddle, or stare in the eyes of someone you have no chemistry with, so look beyond the physical attraction and try to establish a deeper connection. When you've developed a spiritual connection with someone *before* sex... the sex that comes later on will merely be a *bonus*. I believe in the 7 Habits of Highly Effective Relationships (according to Chey B). This requires your partner to be 1) Respectful 2) Loving 3) Honest 4) Trustworthy 5) Loyal 6) Supportive 7) A great communicator. With these key things, your relationship will be destined for greatness.

Since we're on the topic, sex shouldn't even be a factor during the "getting to know each other" process because the focus should be on spending time getting to know each other. The beauty of life and love is... not always knowing what's going to happen next. Look at sex as a way of saving the best for last. Develop a solid friendship with your potential mate, and figure out if he possesses *The 7 Habits of Highly Effective*

Relationships. While getting to know the guy and spending time with him, you will develop a *spiritual* connection or disconnection even. With that spiritual connection intact, the *sexual* connection that comes along with a marriage will be all the more special. The old saying goes "Good things come to those who wait."

After waiting to enjoy one another on a deeper level of spirituality (*sex*), you will have built up such uncontrollable feelings for one another, and once you release it, you will have taken your relationship to a whole new level. After proving your love through the sanctity of marriage, it becomes clear that you genuinely love, care, and value this person. At this point, you'll feel more comfortable with being vulnerable and communicating any problems you may face throughout the relationship. If, for example there's something that your partner isn't doing right in the bedroom, you can work on it *together* and make your sexual experience even better. Practice makes perfect! For better results in your relationship, start from the inside, and work your way out! This practice adds value to your relationship and helps you to avoid getting stuck in a sexually charged relationship that lacks substance.

Men enjoy earning their keep, and they place more value in things they're required to earn. Giving a man sex with no strings is like a boss giving an employee a bonus he hasn't rightfully earned. While a man may appreciate you for giving him your body, he won't value you as much as he would have, if he *earned* the privilege. When you start your relationship off with sex... every encounter you have with one another will be sex driven, and sex will be the only thing he looks forward to. He instead should be looking forward to getting to know you and getting better acquainted.

When you start things off with sex, you give up what he considers to be the highest level of achievement with a woman; not to mention, you'll have missed out on the opportunity to get close to his heart. A man will without a doubt show you who he is after sex, and that may or may not be a good thing. After you give a man sex with no strings, he won't feel obligated to get to know you or allow you to get to know him because it was never a *requirement*. Now you're stuck with a man you're physically connected to, but spiritually and emotionally, he is completely disconnected from you; leaving you feeling *worth less*.

One of the purposes behind the idea of *waiting until marriage* is for you to enjoy the pleasures of sex, but with the one person that you truly love. By being monogamous, you reduce your risk of becoming pregnant by someone who feels they have no obligation to you, being infected by STDs, but more importantly it shows that you value yourself and the relationship you have with your partner. Waiting for sex seems foreign to men today because so many women give them sex right away without requiring anything at all. Men *are* interested in being married, but so many women fail the *wife material* test by giving him too much too soon without any requirements.

When a man is looking for sex, he'll place high value in a woman's outer beauty, but when a man is looking for a wife, he'll place even higher value in a woman's inner beauty. The way for a woman to find a man of substance is to simply *be* a woman of substance.

Focus on being the best woman you can be in every aspect of your life and quality men will inevitably take notice. When a man sees a woman who knows how to take care of herself and others, this is indication of how she could potentially treat *him*. The same principle holds true for the *Diva* who is full of herself and can think of no one but herself; this type of spirit may attract men who are interested in sex, but might repel men who are interested in finding a wife!

There's more to life than having mind blowing sex in abundance, and if you're interested in having a relationship that provides more than a sexual experience, plant the seeds and watch them grow. It's important that any and every relationship have *chemistry* for starters; from there it's simply a matter of where both parties are positioned in life. Being emotionally, spiritually, and financially stable will play a huge role in whether a not a man is ready, able, and willing to commit. So be sure to get to know as much about his position in his own life, before giving him a position in yours. Begin your relationship with *friendship*, and if things don't work out *romantically*, you can at the very least, leave with what you started out with. Every person you allow into your life should be an asset to your life, not a liability; choose wisely!

Make Him Earn His Title

A "relationship" is any union that connects a person or persons. From the moment you meet & connect with someone, you now have a "relationship". The titles of *some* relationships need to actually be communicated, while *others* don't. In order for there to be a clear understanding of a romantic relationship though, both parties should at some point communicate and *define* exactly what it is. Whenever someone earns a new position in your life, they should be given a *title*. When parents give birth to a boy, they call him "son". When a couple gets married, they call one another husband and wife. These titles help identify their roles in each other's lives.

Anytime you allow a man to earn a significant place in your life, he should be given a title that publicly identifies his position. The key piece to this puzzle is making him *earn* a position/title, as opposed to *giving* him a position/title. When a man earns his position, that's indication that he's put in the necessary work that you required him to do, and he's shown you his worth. A man who is given a position/title hasn't necessarily done anything to earn his keep, he's just *around*. There are millions of men in the world, and you only need one. Never focus on a man who isn't focused on you! Give your time, energy, and effort to a man who has and still is proving that he wants to be a part of your life.

Men are natural born hunters; they like to be the aggressors and initiate things that interest them. Being handed things for free takes away the fun in the hunt, and it makes him feel like less than a man because he hasn't earned his keep. With this in mind, know that a quality man of substance does not want to be approached by a woman, asked out on a date, offered a relationship title, or proposed to for marriage. These are things that men want to do on their own, when they're ready, and with the person of their choice. The best way for you to get a man to approach you, date you, commit to you, and marry you is by *showing* him you're worth it. Showing your worth simply means that you are focusing on being the best woman you can be; all the while, you are being *still*, until a man asks you to move into his life.

When you first meet a guy, and you're making his acquaintance, make mental notes of the way he carries himself and the way he approaches you. After evaluating all you can about this individual, make a decision whether or not the relationship should end *there*, or if he's sparked your interest enough to take things further. Always remember that it's great for a woman to set the tone, but you want the man to take the lead and go after what *he* wants. If he asks you for your number, that's a great sign that he would like to reconnect with you after the initial conversation. If he asks you out on a date, that's great, because now it's evident that he sees you as someone he would like to invest time, energy, effort, and money into.

After talking to this gentleman for some time, and you've determined that he's worth giving more of your time to, then by all means, go ahead and entertain the possibility of beginning a friendship. If you're not satisfied with his personality, character, spirituality, or finances, then there's no obligation; you can put an end the association at any time with no hard feelings. This is what getting to know a person is all about; there's a position that needs to be filled and you're interviewing qualified candidates. A qualified candidate is someone who is able and/or willing to match/exceed everything that you're already doing for yourself. With this in mind, you don't want to put out "ads" for an opening, but you instead want to interview the men who come directly *to* you to apply.

Time and money are two things that are very important to a man, so it's a great idea to sit back and observe just how much of both he's willing to invest in you. Now if *you* take the lead and make all of the suggestions on *what* to do and *when* to do it, you'll be unable to measure just how serious he is about you, because he's not acting on his *own* accord. Allow a man to take the initiative, call you, and arrange for a date or outing, while you sit back and enjoy being a woman. When you know your role this early in the relationship, there will be no confusion on the roles that should be played later on in the relationship.

Men enjoy being single because it gives them the space and opportunity to be independent and strengthen his independence. Being in a relationship requires interdependence, and he knows he'll be a much greater asset to you if he's successful during his independence first. Having someone depend on you is a huge responsibility, and he'll only feel comfortable accepting *if* he is ready. When he's ready, he will show you through his actions.

Men are cold/hard on the outside, but warm and soft on the inside. You'll know you're getting closer to a man's heart when he starts to show you his softer side (i.e. the things that are most important to him). The things that mean the world to a man are his family, his time/money, and his dreams. When a man introduces you to important people in his life (i.e. his mother, the females in his family, or his children), this is a sign that he wants you to *see* his life so that you can decide if you want to be *in* his life. When a man invests his *time/money* into you that means that he's potentially interested in forming a partnership, and gaining a long-term return on his investment. When a man shares his dreams with you, that's indication that he is ready to open up and let you in, and that he's not afraid to be vulnerable.

As a woman, you can set the tone by not making yourself 100% available to him. By doing this, you'll prompt him to take action, and perhaps seek out a more concrete position in your life. When you give a man too much too soon, he'll get comfortable and start to take you for granted. You can avoid being taken for granted by keeping yourself busy with your *own* life, until he decides to make you an official part of his. You're not giving up on him; you're simply pulling back a little so that you can measure whether he sees you as *potential* or just a *convenience*.

If the calls become less frequent, the texts become non-existent, and the dates are long gone, then it's quite clear that he's not that into you, or he's not ready to be in a relationship with you. If on the other hand, he's still calling, texting, and showing interest, then this is great indication that he still sees you as someone of value. If he's genuinely interested in you and he's ready for a commitment, he will make the decision to be more exclusive with you, and you'll be the first to know. Your "standoffish" behavior will be just the *push* he needs to ask for exclusivity.

It's up to *you* to not give away free benefits to men who don't commit to you. If you don't make commitment a requirement, men will opt to have a friendship with benefits for as long as you'll allow them to, or until they feel threatened by another man whose showing interest in you. A man will do and say anything to get between a woman's legs, so it's *your* job to set standards, and have requirements in order for him to get there, if a commitment is what you seek. You'll know you're both in a relationship when he asks you to be exclusive, and when he treats you as if you're exclusive.

Get Over Your Ex

I first want you to know that it is perfectly normal to miss your ex (even if he treated you badly). He's the one you've gotten close to, the one you've given your body to, introduced to your family, shared special moments with, grown with, etc. It's hard to let go of someone who's gotten so close to your heart. But it's certainly possible! Think about ALL the ex's before this one. Do you miss them? No! I think not! So what happened? Time elapsed! You met someone new! You moved on with your life! These are all a *part* of the steps you need to take.

First, you have to keep yourself busy with something called *Life*! If you sit at home doing nothing, you'll be constantly reminded of how *lonely* you are, how much you miss your ex, and how much you want to have someone *there*. And that's what this is *really* about! You miss the comfort he gave you, and the convenience of having someone *there* for you. It's not necessarily about *him*, because it could've been *anybody*! He just happens to be the person you're most comfortable being vulnerable around (at the time), and you're afraid of starting over. These feelings shall come to pass!

When I say keep yourself busy, I'm talking things like creating a brand new music playlist, cleaning out your refrigerator, washing your car, painting your living room, going to work as usual, etc. Do things that will free your mind of *him*! Invite your girls over for moral support; it's great to have a good support system/people you can talk to so that you can release your thoughts and feelings. Make sure though that these friends aren't hurt/angry/bitter women themselves, because chances are, they'll advise you simply to forget about him and go right back to the dating scene which is exactly what you *don't* want to do. Now is the time to reflect on what just happened, what's happening currently, and what's getting ready to happen in your future.

Now... if you there's no marriage and you have no kids with your ex, enjoy the good times, cherish the memories, but by God, let him remain an ex *Forever*! If you backtrack, you're simply prolonging the inevitable. Your relationship should end in the same way that it began, and that's with a *conversation*. When you break up with him (or vice versa), have a face-to-face conversation so that you both can get out any and everything you need/want to say. Take as much time as you need (in that one sitting), and make this the *last* conversation that you have together so that you can officially get him out of your system. Do not avoid this step or else he will have a *reason* to contact you and he won't stop until he gets this closure.

You owe it to one another to bring closure to the relationship, so handle the break-up and your ex with dignity and respect. This step will allow you to free yourself of any guilt or any animosity you may have towards him. Talking about all of the issues you had in your relationship with him will allow you to see more clearly why you need to move on. You guys can be cordial, peaceful, and respectful to one another whenever you bump into each other, but outside of that, there's no need for any further contact. You don't have to be the best of friends, but do end things on a friendly basis. It's a *break up*! You don't have to be sworn enemies.

So now we've established that there should be no communication between you two, and there's definitely no *sex*. You can't get over your ex if you're still lying up under him. Many times when we stay in relationships, the sex is the *one* thing that we always agree upon, so while you're in this emotional state, don't confuse your lust with love. Being sexually involved with your ex will only prolong the inevitable, so don't allow yourself to get caught up in the mix. Make up sex is always great because you're taking all of your aggression and channeling it into that one moment of passion. Unfortunately, this is a temporary high and you'll be back to reality shortly thereafter. To avoid a prolonged break-up, stay out of his bed and keep him out of yours!

Keep your mind occupied and off of your ex by doing things for yourself (i.e. massage, manicure, pedicure, join a gym and start working out, start to cook more, read self-help books for motivation/inspiration, talk to your family & friends, etc. Remember, this is only one man and one break up; don't make this out to be the end of the world! If it didn't work out, it didn't work out! It's ok to move on and find someone you can *really* grow with. Relationships are all about *growth*! Yes, the sex was good and he was attractive, and everybody liked him, etc... But *you* couldn't grow with him! So don't continue to stunt your growth! MOVE ON!

When you're fresh out of a failed relationship with someone, the last thing you want to do is jump right back into the dating scene. Use this time to find yourself, and heal from the emotional distress caused by this previous relationship. Taking a spiritual journey after a break-up allows you to take a deep look at yourself, and the things you need to work on in order to make your next relationship a success. Men can sense a woman who's been broken, and they use that knowledge to take advantage of her vulnerable state. If you want to avoid being hurt all over again, take the time to regroup and come back as a better you!

Take as much time as you need to heal your broken heart. Reflect on the good times that you shared with your ex, and value the experiences you shared. Also reflect on the bad times, and use this to remind you of why you made the decision to move on. This healing process is about getting you back to a place where you're able to love and be loved again, so allow time to take its course. You can't move onto the next, until you're through with your ex!

Now here's where it gets fun. While you're doing all these things for yourself, you'll begin to smile more, you'll feel better about yourself, and you'll be *glowing*! The men who cross your path will be on you like a magnet! And you don't have to jump to the opportunities that come your way... just use this fuel to further validate that your ex isn't the only person that can "make you feel good". *You* can make you feel good, and there's a world of other men who will compete for that same opportunity. Then suddenly... that ex doesn't look so good anymore.

Sex Before Marriage

Although birth and sex are typically what men view as a woman's most valued treasures, a woman's "heart & mind" has the most influence. Her ability to use her mind to maintain control over men and situations are simply amazing, but only if/when you realize the gift that you have, and use it to *remain* in control. You have more to fear from dealing with a man who wants access to your mind than your body. A man who wants access to your body is clearly seeking physical pleasure. A man who wants access to your mind is after *more*! How much more is totally ambiguous.

Even if a man doesn't value your body for what it's truly worth, then as a woman *you* should. A man can't get inside of you unless you let him, so if you're going to allow a man to come into your personal space and be intimate with you, then it should be with a man you love, trust, and respect and who reciprocates these same things. When you involve yourself with a man who loves you, respects you, and is trustworthy, you establish a special bond that holds *value*. When you're committed to someone who values you, you strengthen your relationships sense of security and increase your chances of having a longer-lasting and more meaningful relationship.

When you develop a spiritual connection with someone prior to sleeping with them, the sex then becomes a *bonus*. If for example, you experience sex with your husband for the first time and you find that it's not as great as you had hoped, you can then create a special bonding experience by sharing details of how you like to be pleased. After communicating what you like to your partner and vice versa, your sex life will be

111

Food, Sex & Peace of Mind

enhanced because you're challenging yourself to do so. You're creating an exclusive physical & spiritual experience with your life partner that cannot be duplicated with anyone, anywhere!

Now that you've both communicated your likes/dislikes, mutual pleasure will become that much easier. You'll love the way he kisses you, the way he touches you, the way he makes love to you, and you'll gain a special appreciation for the way *he* romances you because you've trained him well. This is the consideration that one has for the person they love, trust, and respect. Love, trust, and respect isn't developed over night and it's not handed out to every Tom, Dick, and Harry. It's *earned*!

And just as love, trust, and respect is earned, the privilege of having sex with you should be earned as well. If you don't set any standards or have any requirements for a man to meet prior to having sex with you, he's likely to sleep with you, and afterwards have total disregard for you, your feelings, and your beliefs because he's lost all respect for you as a *lady*. He's already reached the ultimate form of pleasure with you and has no reason to return unless he wants more sex with no strings.

When you give your body to someone you're not married to, they have no real obligation to you. No matter your relationship status, having sex in general makes you vulnerable to pregnancy, STDs, and other fatal diseases. A man who has no obligation to you is likely to flee if/when the two of you face adversity, simply because he's afraid and doesn't want any serious involvement with you. When you've taken the time to get to know a man and have made things official through marriage, you can rest assured and feel secure in knowing that your husband will be there to help you get through these times.

Being married is a badge of honor that you should be proud to wear, and after you've achieved it, you can then enjoy the love of your life and explore every possibility there is with them until your heart is content. Being married means that you've found someone you love, honor, and cherish, and are willing to commit to no matter how good or bad things get. You only get one body, so making love with the person you believe in your heart only has eyes for you will be quite refreshing. There is no-guarantee that your significant other will not stray away, but having faith that they won't and working towards living up to *your* promise is what will make this journey worthwhile.

Life is about building relationships and leaving behind legacies. When you give your body to a man who hasn't earned that privilege, you leave behind a legacy of being a woman who's fast, easy, and doesn't respect herself. As a woman, you should never want to be remembered by *anyone* in that light. You have a bright future ahead of you and you don't want your past to come back and haunt you. Always carry yourself with dignity and respect, place value on your body and only give yourself to a man who is deserving of it.

Chapter Five

Marriage is Forever

20 Steps To Getting/Keeping The Man You Want

Marriage is meant to be a life-long commitment, so it deserves every bit of special attention when preparing yourself for it. Before taking this step towards a happy life with someone else, you want to make sure you have a happy life as an individual. Marriage isn't only about having a man who will take care of you; it's also about you being ready, willing, and able to take care of him. These 20 steps will serve as an excellent guide for preparing yourself for a happy, healthy relationship, and help you work towards a marriage.

Step 1: Self-evaluation- (i.e. How do you feel about the person you are inside and out?) You have to love yourself before you love someone else.

Step 2: Presentation- Always present yourself as the person you want to be known and remembered as. Men are visual and will evaluate you 1st based on your appearance and also by the way you carry yourself.

Step 3: The Introduction- Remember you're a lady! Maintain control! Just give a guy you're interested in "the look" & he will come right over & initiate convo. This will show your submissive side, while allowing him to take the lead.

Step 4: Friendship- There will be plenty of time for sex, but if you want a future with this man, 1st get to know him and find out if you even *like* the guy. Friendship is the key to romance!

Step 5: Dating- Focus on the man who focuses on you, but in the meantime, keep your options open. Date multiple people at once.

116

Step 6: Sex- Friendship doesn't come with *benefits*. Benefits come with a commitment. If he wants sex, your relationship has to be exclusive. Know your worth!

Step 7: Commitment- You've been dating this guy for a while, the chemistry is great, and you've established a great friendship, and you're ready to take the next step. Go ahead and make it official! Let *him* ask to be exclusive with you.

Step 8: Incorporate The 7 Habits of Highly Effective Relationships (according to Chey B.) Those habits are: Respect, Love, Trust, Support, Loyalty, Honesty & Communication.

Step 9: Consistency- Everything you brought to the table in the beginning should not only remain, but it should get better. Never stop competing for your partner's love and affection.

Step 10: Share your world! Introduce your partner to any/everyone who is important in your life. This shows him that you want him to be a part of it. Even a man wants to feel special.

Step 11: Space- Allow each other just enough room to breathe, but not enough room to leave. Give yourselves the opportunity to miss one another.

Step 12: Growth- If you want to grow as a couple, it's important that you do things "as a couple". Not all the time, but most of the time.

Step 13: Secrets- If you can't be open and honest with your partner, you are not ready for a relationship. Stay single until you're ready to be vulnerable. Being in a relationship means that you're a team! Keep secrets *with* your partner, not *from* your partner.

Step 14: Male friends- Platonic friendship is an

oxymoron! All men have a motive! Friendship is the *key* to romance and men use this approach to get close to a woman's heart, mind, and body! Your partner should be your one and only male friend! Keep the peace in your relationship by dismissing them all!

Step 15: Single friends- You're in a relationship now! From time to time, your single friends will invite you out to share *their* world; invite them in to come and share *yours* instead. Use this as an opportunity to show your single friends the value in being in a committed relationship while also strengthening yours.

Step 16: Engagement- Don't waste countless years of your life hoping, wishing, and praying for a marriage proposal. A man knows from the very beginning whether he wants to marry you or not. Expect a proposal no later than year two or three.

Step 17: Wedding Plans- Communicate with your partner, set a time-line for the activities leading up to the wedding, as well as a tentative wedding date, work together and find a way to include both parties' family and friends to help assist. Start planning the wedding within weeks after the engagement.

Step 18: Getting Married- After 2-3 years of following the rules of relationships, you're certain that you want to spend the rest of your life with this man. Go for it! You are about to become an official team; you are *one*! Let no one and nothing come between you two. You marriage should be impenetrable and inseparable! Always protect and value this union!

Step 19: Moving in- You're about to find out *new* things about your husband. Don't be alarmed; simply observe, take notes, and prepare to make any necessary adjustments.

Step 20: Relationship Turmoil- Remember all the steps you took to get to where you are, and know that your marriage is worth fighting for. Never stop loving one another. Marriage is forever!

Know How Long To Wait For A Proposal

People sometimes tend to use relationships for everything short of building a future with someone. Relationships are *optional* so if you're not ready, willing, or able to commit to someone, don't! The sole purpose of being in a relationship is to have the *added* support from someone you're romantically interested in, with the potential to grow! If there's no potential to grow, there's no sense in being in an exclusive relationship with someone; you can do bad or good all by yourself.

When you first meet someone, you evaluate them based on their appearance, their character, morals/values, etc., and from there you can decide whether or not this person is worth giving more of your time. Once you've determined he is worth giving more of your time, all you have to do is simply give him *more* of your time. Do this until he has proven to be someone to be taken seriously and considered for a position that will allow him to be closer to your heart, and to the people who are important in your life.

Side note: Before you give a man your time, make sure he has a steady source of income. If he can't afford to take care of himself *now*, he won't be able to afford courting you, he won't be able to afford a ring to propose, and unless something drastically changes with his finances, he won't be able to afford the wedding of your dreams within the next 2-3 years. If somehow he miraculously comes up with the money within 2-3 years, chances are he won't be willing to spend all he has on *you*. He will take care of his *own* priorities *first*. The idea is to get married "one time" in your life, so

120

don't sell yourself short by getting married at a courthouse or in Vegas just because this man doesn't have his life together. If you marry a broke man, you can expect to have a *broke* marriage. Not quite the "Happily Ever After" you imagined eh?

While you're getting to know this person, dating, etc., you'll also be busy with your own personal life; whatever that might entail (i.e. Work, school, kids, etc.). Days, weeks, and months will go by before he's earned his place in your heart. If at this point, you feel comfortable enough to take things further, grant him the opportunity to ask for a commitment. You don't have to "wait" for him to ask. Simply keep yourself busy so he'll be prompted to ask you for more exclusivity. When you withhold special privileges from a man, he will do *anything* to receive favor from you (including marriage), especially if he considers you to be a woman of substance.

Three months is more than enough time to determine whether or not a man should or should not become your significant other, so at this point, make the decision to either keep him around or keep it moving *now*. You do this by making yourself less and less available to him, which will prompt *him* to take the lead. If you express to him through words that you want more, you're likely to scare him off and make him change his mind about you. Instead, use a subtle approach by simply removing yourself from the picture so he'll work harder to get you *back* in the picture. Think of relationships as a big game of *chess*! You study your target, plan your moves, and always keep your mate in check!

Food, Sex & Peace of Mind

After deciding that you'd like to get more serious with one another and it's established that you're now a couple, continue to get to know one another while still living your lives. Be sure not to smother one another; give each other enough room to breathe, but not enough room to leave. Men of substance are secure in themselves, they are independent and enjoy keeping their independence, so be sure to establish that you too are capable of enjoying life on your own, and at the same time enjoying his company when he's around. Coming off as too needy or clingy early on in the relationship is a sure fire way to send a man running for the hills.

Throughout the 1st year of being together, you will experience a birthday, Valentine's Day, Halloween, Thanksgiving, Christmas, New Years, and an entire summer's worth of excitement! If this person is someone you are interested in growing with, there will be no question in your mind that you will want to spend each and every one of the upcoming Holiday's *together*. If this is the way you're mutually feeling about one another, it would be a nice touch to invite your partner to family gatherings and introduce one another to the people who are most important in your life. This is a great sign of vulnerability and growth!

After you've introduced him to the people who are most important in your life, be sure to get your partner's feedback on what he thinks of your family, and also get your family's feedback on what they think of your partner. Both opinions are equally important so listen carefully to the feedback they give you. Your family has nothing invested in your relationship... but they genuinely care about *you* and your well being, so treasure the things they tell you that they see in the man you're with.

If your family *who loves and cares about you* gets the sense that there's something unsettling about your partner's character, and they feel as though he's not a good fit, it's a good idea to take those feelings into consideration when deciding your future with him. This doesn't have to be *the* determining factor, but certainly *a* factor in your decision-making. Often times when we're in love, we don't see or think clearly, and we're blinded by our current emotional state; people on the outside looking in sometimes have a clearer vision of our current situation because they are not emotionally involved, so value their opinions.

No matter how many men who come and go from your life, your family will always be there; however your family will be reluctant to help you in the future if you don't appreciate the help that they're offering *now*. Staying in a relationship that everyone around you views as unhealthy will affect the way your family views your partner, your relationship, and *your* character from that point on (if you stay in that relationship). Also, your family comes *first*, so if your partner has a problem with your family, then *you* should have a problem with *him*. Weigh the pros and cons and decide on your own accord what's best for you. No matter who's giving the feedback, never disregard the feelings of the people who love and care for you; they are there to help!

So now one full year has gone by and if you've survived the Holidays, survived meeting the family, and survived each other, then you're definitely on the right track. In a full year's time, the seasons will have changed, you'll have learned so much about your partner, and now it's time for a *pause*! After one year of your life has gone by… ask yourself how do you *now* feel about your partner? Are you still excited to see him? Are you still interested in growing? Is he being consistent with the behavior he's exhibited from the beginning? If so, continue to enjoy this person's company, and continue to do things that will bring you closer together. If you're not happy, *this* is the time to reevaluate.

Throughout this 2nd year, those Holiday's will have rolled back around again, and if your family liked the man you brought around them the first time, they will be delighted to see that you're still with him. Only this time, your family will sense that the two of you are getting serious about one another, so they'll want to know if marriage and babies are in the near future. He will love the fact that your family accepts him and feels as though he's worthy of such privileges, so these honorable mentions will be on his mind and on his heart. And he's also aware that *you* heard these mentions as well. After hearing such accolades, he'll feel a little bit of pressure to do *something*… and soon. Otherwise, he can look forward to holding his head low in shame the next time he faces your family if there's been no progression. A relationship should not be a flat line; it should always be on the path of growth!

Side note: It's very important to be family oriented when you're in a relationship, because it establishes what a person values (or the lack thereof). It becomes a matter of *pride* after a certain amount of years go by and your family, friends, and co-workers are not seeing any growth in you or your relationship. They may not say anything after a certain amount of years, because by then they will have accepted the fact that the two of you aren't going anywhere... and they'll simply stop inquiring/caring about what your future holds. The only people left to realize that the relationship isn't going anywhere is the people who are actually in the relationship...*You* and *him*!

After year two, his feelings for you should be crystal clear! If at this point he is in a comfortable place financially, and he still feels the same way about you as he felt in the beginning, he will want to do something to take your relationship to the next level because he wants for this experience to continue on and remain exclusive. On the other hand, if at this point he isn't considering popping the question, or feels differently about you, then he'll probably be content remaining your boyfriend until one of you can't take it anymore. If this is the case, cut your losses and end the relationship with him (even if it hurts).

Marriage is a very tough decision for a man to make, so if the relationship is still healthy and you feel as though he's possibly considering marrying you, be sure not to give him any reason to change his mind. It's during these stages of marriage consideration, that his tolerance will be at an all-time low and he'll be subconsciously *looking* for a reason not to pop the question, so don't give him one. Marriage (to a man) can be quite intimidating so whatever you do... do not pressure him into making this decision. Do not even *mention* the words "marriage" around him unless you're intentionally trying to get rid of him. It's already been established during the getting to know you process that you desire to get married, and you can show him in subtle ways that you will not stick around without a marriage.

It takes a man a great deal of courage to walk up to a woman and simply say hello, so if you can imagine, it will take a man even more strength, courage, and self-assurance to propose marriage. While you're in a relationship with a man, always be his support system so that he can feel 100% comfortable coming to you and talking to you about anything on his heart and mind. If throughout the relationship you've proven to be an asset to his life, he will want to give you the title that you rightfully deserve, and will be more open to making it a reality.

Marriage is a life changing decision and a serious commitment, and it will take him a little bit of time to think. It's not that he's not sure about you; he's simply a bit nervous about the change he's getting ready to experience. A marriage will require him to share his assets, his living space, his last name, and pretty much his entire world! This is something that he has to run through his "board of trustees" before making it official (i.e. His mother, his father, his siblings, and his boys for their approval). If you've already met these people and have made a good impression, you're in good standings.

You can rush a man into bed, but one thing that's for certain is that you can't rush a man into a relationship or a marriage, so while you wait, continue to be the best woman you can be. The last thing you want is for a man to marry you as a result of an ultimatum. If your goal is to be married and the man you're with doesn't want to be married, then maybe that's not the man you should be spending years of your life with. Go where you're celebrated, not tolerated! If you're with a man who enjoys being around you, loves you to death, and wants to build a future with you, you can expect a marriage proposal between years 2-3.

If its past year 3 and you still haven't gotten the ring, then you should take a look at your life and your relationship, and reevaluate your situation. Some men can go a life time simply being in a relationship that offers friendship and benefits. He could care less about a title because he's already getting everything that he feels a marriage could possibly offer. It's common for a man to use an engagement as a way to keep the benefits flowing, with no real intentions on investing in a wedding, or going through with a marriage. Instead of being mesmerized by the *words* "will you marry me", play close attention to his *actions* and ask yourself, "Does his actions show that he's interested in marrying me? Or is he leading me solely with his words?" Never listen to a man's words... always follow his actions!

If you agree to a marriage proposal, do so not just for the sake of saying, "I got the ring!", but because you've found a man who loves you, cares for you, and values having you in his life. If a man doesn't see value in you from the beginning, let that be the end. Do not allow a man to take years of your life deciding whether or not he feels you're worth marrying. This is a trick that men use to string women along. A man knows the role he wants for a woman to play in his life before he even meets her! Never settle for less; always settle for more!

What Men of Substance Look for in a Wife

For ages, many men have valued women solely based on their physical beauty, ignoring the possibility of exploring anything more. Some of these powers include a woman's ability to seduce a man into doing any and everything she wants him to. This is partially true; for a man will allow a woman to persuade him into doing *only* what he is *willing* to do. The things that are off limits will remain off limits unless *he* decides she is worthy of such privileges. It's easy for a woman to get a man into bed, but what's challenging is getting a man to commit to a relationship or propose marriage. This is where we cross over into the realm of what a man *truly* values.

Sometimes, it takes a man years to learn that not everything that glitters is gold. That beautiful face and a phenomenal body doesn't automatically equate to a warm, loving heart, or a woman of good character. For years he'll follow his eyes and ignore his heart, struggling endlessly to turn that sexy, seductive sex slave into a beautiful, sensual, wholesome lady whom he can be proud to take home to his mother. All the while, he bypasses the beautiful, sensual, wholesome women at the library, at the grocery store, or at church because he doesn't see the value in being with *that* type of woman, but this is also because he hasn't learned to value himself and figure out his *own* worth.

After a young man gets out of a long-term relationship with his parents, one of the first things he looks to do is find himself and figure out his own way. One of the things that are forbidden in most parents'

128

household is having the opposite sex over for company. So now that he's left the nest, one of the first things on his mind is to get sex and lots of it! He's filling a void that's been missing for the past 18 years of his life, and he's going to indulge until his heart is content.

Despite the years of teachings received from his parents, the last thing on his mind is being a mature, responsible adult. Breaking away from the parents is a man's time to *be a man* and explore the world through his own eyes! While he's in this young, wild, immature, and promiscuous stage of his life, he will look to associate with women who are *just* like him (i.e. Young, wild, immature, and promiscuous). He's not interested in finding a woman of substance just yet, because he *himself* hasn't become anyone of substance.

At first glance, it may appear to a lady that "H**s be winning!" because all of the men seem to flock to the women who are fast and easy, but this is only true if you view giving up free sex with no commitment, to every Tom, Dick, and Harry" *winning*! These women are only valued for as long as they're spreading their legs. Outside of the bedroom, h**s are worth less, they're only worth more to the men who solely value sex without a commitment. Do not be discouraged; these are the men you want to avoid anyway! Quality over quantity!

These very same women who give up years of their lives sleeping with men without any requirements will come to find that they are merely *stepping stones* for these men. A man who is on a journey to finding himself will encounter many different jobs, many different fashion trends, and many different women long before finding his *true* identity. As the years roll by and a man matures, you'll notice he starts to do away with old fashion trends, he moves on to better paying jobs/careers, seeks out higher paying positions, and associates more closely with higher quality women. Those things were all *stepping stones* that reflected the person that he was at that particular point in his life, but will no longer be present in his future.

While strippers and porn stars have amazing visual and sexual qualities, they are what men consider to be a *fantasy*, and he wants to keep his fantasy and his reality totally *separate*. He'll come to watch her perform merely for entertainment, he'll spend a fair amount of money on her, and he'll even engage in a sexual rendezvous or two, but after the climax, it's back to reality. His *reality* is work, family, friends, and life; he finds pleasure in experiencing a fantasy from time to time, but he doesn't want this side of him exposed in his regular everyday life. What he expects from a stripper and/or porn star is *entertainment*, nothing more, nothing less!

To *settle down* is to have experienced all that there is to experience up until the point of exhaustion, and reaching a level of contentment. With this in mind, it will take a man *years* of having loads of sex, with an abundance of women, with no strings attached before he is ready to genuinely and sincerely settle down with just *one* woman. The same applies to his financial stability; it may take a man years of spending frivolously, making costly mistakes, and not valuing a dollar before he finally decides for himself to be more financially responsible. No matter whether its money, fashion, or women, a man has to surpass certain milestones in his life before he's ready to become a man of substance and experience a shift in values.

Before a man even thinks of settling down, he has to be emotionally available; meaning there is no one and nothing in his life preventing him from opening his heart to you. Finances (or the lack thereof), are one of the key factors in determining whether a not a man entertains a woman, and it also narrows down *which* woman a man will choose. If he's not financially stable, he again will bypass the women of *substance* and seek out the women of *suspense* because most quality women require more of an investment. It's not that a man is not interested in quality, but at this point in his life, he's unable to afford it, so in the meantime, he'll entertain the woman who will settle for little to nothing.

Again, it may *seem* as though "H**s be winning!" but the relationship a man has with h**s are a *temporary* solution to a temporary problem. Sometimes a man will get into a relationship with a woman who has no requirements as a way to save money on rent, get free sex, meals, and other resources. They know from the start that they don't want a future with this woman, but the *opportunist* in them, says, "Hey, it's better to get free sex, meals, and a roof over my head than to struggle alone." While that may be his initial plan of action, what happens is he gets *caught up*, gets comfortable, and ends up staying far longer than he planned. He's now fallen in love with a woman he doesn't value, hasn't thoroughly planned an exit strategy, and is now angry with *her* because *he* has fallen in love with a woman he never imagined he would get emotionally attached to. His plan was supposed to be "strictly business", but in the end it blew up in his face!

If it hasn't already, that relationship will turn verbally and possibly physically abusive. Not only will he hate *you* for being who you are, but also he'll secretly hate himself for being who *he* is and landing himself in that position. He'll make himself feel better about being a man of poor character by channeling all of his anger and negative energy towards *you*! Had he been focused on his own independence, he would've never even considered *this* type of woman, he instead, would have gotten himself emotionally and financially stable, and he will have then sought out a woman who matches everything that he is. When you seek out a relationship while you're at your worst, you'll find yourself matched with an individual who also is at their worst (on one level or another).

It's easy for a woman to *get* a man through sex, but she'll never be able to *keep* him through sex. Sex only keeps the men who *only* value sex around. If you're looking for a man who values more, you'll have to present yourself as a woman who offers more. Once a man makes up in his mind who you are and where he wants you to be in his life, that's exactly where you'll stay. This could mean you're his *fantasy*, his *reality*, or his *resource*.

You want your future husband to be a man who has already established who he is, and where he wants to be in life. No matter how long it takes him, or what he had to go through to get there, you want your man to be spiritually, financially, and emotionally stable. A man who is independent, has taken a spiritual journey, and has experienced life will at some point have a strong desire for something *more*! When he reaches this point in his life, he will bypass all of his past conquests because he's been there and done that, and he'll look for that woman of substance; the woman he's been ignoring his entire life.

He's now ready to be a man of integrity, a man of honor, a man of substance, and start building his legacy. As an independent man, he's now interested in finding an independent woman whose interested in coming together and gaining interdependence. He realizes now that he can do *anything* by himself, but he can do *more* with the help of a quality woman by his side. His ideal woman would be someone who can be an asset to his life; someone who knows her worth and who only entertains quality men of *substance*. A woman who will take her time, get to know a man, value her body before giving it to him, and set standards/requirements before giving herself to him.

He finds this woman by simply *observing* how she carries herself, and how she handles other people. This is the same approach he used when finding a whore when he was younger; he would target women who have low self-esteem and are desperate for *any* man to be a part of their lives. Now that he's grown and matured, he's looking for *substance*, not *suspense*. This time around he'll be looking for a woman not only with his eyes, but with his heart! Now that he's all grown up, he's learned to value himself, women, and relationships, and he's ready for a serious commitment.

A man will treat you the way you treat yourself, so if you're a woman who doesn't carry herself with dignity and respect, he will degrade you in the same way you're degrading yourself. If you're someone who helps people to better themselves, he'll see you as warm, compassionate, loving, caring, and giving, and he'll treat you that way. Contrary to popular belief, the key to finding a good man isn't by looking for him, but instead, taking a journey to find *you.* A woman who exhibits poor character automatically disqualifies *herself* from being a candidate for a relationship or marriage. If you possess the qualities that men look for in a wife, he will gladly seek you out as soon as he is ready for that level of commitment.

The Power of Submission

Submission is a great quality to have and use in a relationship. The man is the king and the woman is the queen, and the sooner both parties understand their roles, the more successful that relationship will be. Ladies, no matter what a man thinks in his mind, at the end of the day *you* are in total control. By submitting to your man, you give him a temporary victory, boosting his ego, and making him feel better about himself as a man. You'll also notice that the more you make him feel better about himself as a man, the more hours he'll put in at work to provide for his beautiful queen, the more housework he'll do to make sure you're happy, and the more he'll want to come home to a place where he's the "King of the jungle".

If you're paying close attention, you'll see that in actuality, *he* is in fact submitting to all of *your* hearts desires (without you even asking). *Your* actions will inspire and motivate him to be the best man he can be not only for *you*, but also for *himself*. This honor of submission by the way should only be given to the man who has earned this privilege through marriage. Your *worth* is determined by the value you add to the lives of *others,* so if you want a man to earn certain privileges by marrying you, you have to *show* him that you're worth marrying by carrying yourself as marriage material.

A man who hasn't yet taken the step of marrying you *also* has to prove himself and show that he's worthy of having you submit to him, and perform other wifely duties. As you grow closer to your partner through dating and getting to know each another, the two of you should exhibit qualities of a good wife and husband, but not yet perform *all* of the actual duties.

Submission isn't as terrible as it may seem, and can be a very powerful weapon in your arsenal. Take for example going out on a date with a guy you like; it's customary for a man to court his woman, so instead of taking charge and planning the date yourself, be submissive, and allow him to take that initiative. Before a date even takes place, hopefully he's taken the time to get to know you, he knows what you like to eat/drink, and things you like to do for fun, so he can use this information to plan accordingly. If allowed, he'll choose a nice place for the two of you to go, schedule a time and a date, and make sure you have a good time. You leave all the hard work up to him while you sit back and enjoy being a woman.

This gesture not only allows you to see what a man can do on his own merit, but it allows *him* to see that you're a woman who knows how to make a man feel like a man! While you're sitting back and enjoying being a woman, you should be taking notes and measuring how (if at all) the man you're dating will fit into your life. When you take matters into your own hands, you'll miss out on a world of information that a man will reveals about himself when he takes his own initiative. Men who lack integrity will sit back and allow you to take full initiative, because what that tells him is, you don't want a man to be in control, and since he's relieved of these duties, he can kick back, relax, and enjoy the free ride!

You see, just about everything a man does revolve around a woman! He works a job, buys nice clothes, decorates his home, stays well-groomed, etc., all so that he can impress a woman. But he's only willing to go the distance for a woman who shows her appreciation, by simply stroking his ego and making him feel good about his accomplishments. It doesn't take much; men are pleased with a simple "Thank you" after he's taken the initiative to plan a nice evening, made sure you're comfortable and entertained, and saw to it that you made it home safely. The more you show your appreciation for his efforts, the better he'll feel as a man and the more likely he'll be willing to do nice things for you again.

Dates are meant to be fun filled and stress free, so don't make it stressful by thinking you *deserve* something from a man simply because you're "pretty". You *deserve* everything you put into a relationship; if you put in nothing, you deserve nothing! If a man has chosen you as a potential candidate for dating, use this opportunity to show him why he made the right choice. If you're not mutually interested in him, there's no sense in entertaining the date in the first place, but if you see yourself being with this person, then Game On!!! *Now* is the time for you to show him that everything he's looking for in a wife is in *you*!

When it comes to men, he already *knows* if you're the woman he wants to marry before he even meets you. He also knows if you're just someone he's going to keep around as a sex slave. If by chance he chooses you and he has the heart to marry you, you don't want to mess it up by not knowing your role as a woman. A lot of women want to married, but don't know how to be wives, and this is one of the main reasons men bypass certain women, and don't consider them for marriage... because they don't make him feel like a man!

Food, Sex & Peace of Mind

No matter who you are, where you're from, or what you do for a living, *you* can eliminate a lot of the tension in a relationship by simply allowing the man to *be* the man! It doesn't matter if you make more money than your man, because if he's your husband, you'll both be sharing all the resources anyway. What a man values is having the ability to do nice things for his woman and having her show her appreciation. As long as he's able to take care of himself, you, and his home, money should never be an issue.

Submission by no means insists that you will become a man's *slave*; No! That's no fun! Submission is simply knowing your role and playing it well. You want your man to know that he is the head of the household, and the leader in the family. By giving him this position he knows he is the man, and he feels great about having you as his woman. Once the two of you know the roles you're supposed to play in the relationship, you can then focus more time and energy on being a team! You want your man to know and understand that *because* he is a man, he is expected to protect and provide; you don't ever want your man to lose sight of that.

As his lady or his *potential* lady, you want to let him know that you are there for him, you love him, you support him, and you appreciate him. Learn to believe in and trust in the man you're giving your time to. Support his decisions and let him lead and take control (if even only for *appearance* sake). A man loves to do things for his woman; it gives him a sense of *purpose* in this world. Always encourage your man to possess the 3P's: Protector, Provider, and Problem solver. If you show a man you don't want or need his help, you make him feel as though he serves no purpose in your life. Continue to give him *purpose*!

Give Each Other Space

There are two rules to love 1) You do it! 2) You don't! It's easy to love someone from a distance because there's no significant time, energy, or effort required to make the relationship work. Anytime you haven't seen someone in a while, there's the *thrill* of being in each other's presence once again, and there's a desire to get caught up to date on things. Space and time apart creates *romance*; the desire to show love and receive love from a person who's been missing from your life.

One of the keys to making romance in a relationship last is to not become *too* familiar, and get stuck in a routine. While it's not important that your significant other knows your each and every move, it is important that when granted this level of freedom and trust, that you honor it by staying true to yourself and true to your partner. Always apply The 7 Habits of Highly Effective People (According to Chey B.) Respect, Love, Honesty, Trust, Loyalty, Support, and Communication. Incorporate these habits and your partner will have no reason to question or doubt the moves you make.

A great way to keep a relationship fresh all the way to the *end* is by being consistent with everything you did in the *beginning*. In the beginning, a man is a gentleman, he honors/respects/treats you like a lady, spends time *apart* and schedules time to be *together*. A lady is warm, loving, caring, supportive, submissive, and is a joy to her man's life. The time spent apart makes the time spent together that much more special. With work, school, and other responsibilities, it's a breath of fresh air to be whisked away from life's harsh realities by a person who is genuinely interested in

140

being with you.

As adults, you're naturally going to have a busy life working, playing, and spending time with the people you care about. With all of these things going on throughout your busy day, it's important that you don't forget to include your significant other in the festivities. A common mistake that many people make once they've "got the girl/guy" is they stop competing for one another's love and affection. The competition (i.e. admirers) never stops coming, and if you don't see to it that your partner is happy, someone *else* will. The best way to remain a couple is to do things as a couple; but it's healthy to do so in moderation.

If both parties are not consistent throughout the relationship, *space* can be your worst enemy. When a man is happy to have you around, he'll also look forward to your return whenever you're gone. When a man *isn't* happy to have you around, he'll look for ways to create space and fill these voids by any means necessary when you're gone. You're a *team* now, so always make sure that *you're* happy, and also make sure that the person you're with is happy. Love should always dwell inside of *you* and inside of your home. When love is lost, your man is bound to go looking elsewhere to find it. Your partner should always feel as though you're a source where he can refuel financially, mentally, spiritually, physically, and emotionally.

Many times we stay in relationships not because we're happy to hold on, but because we're afraid to let go. Once you stop loving you'll start hating. Once you stop hating, you'll start loving. Never stop loving yourself, and never stop loving your partner. Work strategically to make sure that your partner enjoys being

Food, Sex & Peace of Mind

with you when you're together, and looks forward to coming back to you when you're apart. Make being *together* the "place to be".

Whenever you and your partner spend time apart, the anticipation to come back together will be the thing that keeps the excitement going. When you give your man something to look forward to, he'll be more focused on what's up *ahead*, rather than what's on the *side*. Life is often an ambiguous journey, so if you're partnered with someone and you're interdependent; make the journey for the both of you as enjoyable as possible. It's a challenge to be able to entertain someone for a long period of time, but that's what comes along with a commitment, so get creative.

Friendship outside of the relationship is also very important because it gives you both something to do when you would like to spend some time *away* from each other. Establish trust between your partner and any of your relevant friends by introducing them early on in the relationship. The friends you associate with are huge reflections of who you are and/or who you aspire to be, so in order to maintain a happy/healthy relationship at home, associate closely with those who are positive influences in your life.

Sometimes starting a *new* life will require *new* friends. If you're in a relationship, cherish the glory days of hanging out with all of your other single friends, and live for *today* by planning for a brighter future with the love of your life. A great way to still stay connected with your single friends is to host gatherings at your home; invite both couples and singles. By inviting your single friends to actually witness your new life "as a couple"; you're granted the opportunity to show them the value in being committed.

Since we're all adults, there's no need for a curfew when your man plans to go out, nor is there a need to constantly call to check up on him once it's been communicated that he's stepping out. *He* should keep in mind though, that you love him, and you're concerned about his well-being, and will miss him while he's gone. If he's going someplace where you're not invited, he should at least be courteous enough to let you know where he's going, who he's going with, and when you should expect him home. This information will make *anyone* feel secure, and he should take pride in knowing that his home and everyone in it is safe and secure.

One of the greatest benefits of being in a relationship is the *companionship*. It feels good to be able to come home to someone you truly love, who you can spend quality time with, and share your world with. Relationships are meant to be experienced *together*, not apart, so spending weeks, months, and years away from one another may cause turmoil. You want to give your partner just enough room to *breathe*, but not enough room to *leave*. Being away from your partner creates space and opportunity, and with that comes the desire to go out and do something with *whoever* will fill that void.

One of the best ways to stay a couple is to do things as a couple. If you'd like to take a nice vacation, plan in advance and budget accordingly so that you and your partner can enjoy a trip *together*. If there's a networking event coming up, let your partner know in advance so that he can mark his calendar and accompany you. If there's a new movie coming out that you'd like to see, invite your partner and make it a date night. You and your man should get in the habit of doing things *with* one another, so that when it's time for you both to do things *alone*, neither party will feel neglected.

The right amount of space and time a part can create the *illusion* of being "without" the person you love, giving you both the opportunity to actually *miss* one another. The anticipation of the return is what helps the romance grow stronger. There's a great chance that your man will get bored and feel smothered if you're constantly around him day in and day out. So much so that he will want to find a source of entertainment *outside* of the home, and *away* from you (for a change). To avoid this, find balance between work, school, other responsibilities, couple's time, and alone time.

A little bit of reverse psychology never hurt either (i.e. encourage your man to go out and hang out with his friends and have fun). Let him know that you'll be at home waiting when he returns and that you actually *want* him to go out and have a good time with his friends. At the end of the night you'll be right back in each other's warm embrace. Create space when there *is* none and you will see and feel the void in the air; you'll look forward to being in your lovers' presence again all thanks to a little time apart.

Always Put Family First

Throughout our journeys in life, we will meet many wonderful people in many different places; some may stay, and some may go. No matter who comes into our lives and who leaves, you should always hold your family dear. We sometimes forget the names of the people we grew up with, the kids we went to school with, the people we used to work with, because they're not a *priority* in our lives. When it comes to family though, you should never forget, exclude, or abandon your blood.

It's great to have a spiritual and emotional connection to other people because it adds more value to the relationship. It's not enough for someone to *know* that you love them; it's important for a person to *hear* that you love them through words, and also be *shown* that you love them through actions. When you have someone that you love, you can be an inspiration to them by *showing* them a little love; it can be simply by saying the words "I love you" or even by giving them a warm hug. These *little* things make *big* differences. Love starts in the home, so be a distributor of love to everyone in your household, and pray that love will always dwell inside of you all. A family that prays together stays together.

Home is where the heart is! The hearts that dwell inside the home should somehow find unity; this means if there is someone in your household is unhappy, or is simply having a bad day, the family should come together and address these issues. The man of the house should be a leader and an inspiration to everyone by governing himself accordingly and inspiring principles. *Everyone* should start their day off feeling great, being inspired to take on the challenges of the world, and looking forward to coming home to a place that feels like paradise. If your home feels like a prison or a nightmare, there's a great chance that the people who live there will want to spend more time everywhere *else* than at home with their family. Make your home feel like an *escape* from the world's harsh realities, instead of a place that reminds them of it.

Everywhere you go and everything you do should be a reflection of who you are and what you represent. When you have a family, you represent *them* as well as *yourself*, so always present yourself in the way you want to be known and remembered as. Carry yourself with dignity and respect when you're around your family, and continue to do the same when you're not. The people you love deserve to have a positive role model who is strong enough and capable of leading a respectable and commendable life; just as you would expect the same representation from them.

If there's anything we have in this world, it's *time*, and you can never be too busy for the family you've created. Your family depends on you, so be sure that you're always there for them. A husband and a wife need each other, children need their parents, and siblings need one another. Without our families, we're left in this world with a bunch of *random* people. Allow the love you have for yourself and the love you have for your family to be the glue that keeps you together for as long as you live.

Being a family requires *teamwork*. Everyone has a role to play and everyone is responsible for doing his or her part in the relationship. The man of the house protects and provides, the woman of the house nurtures and supports, and the children serve as aids to both parents. A family *divided* stays weak, but a family *united* stays strong! Encourage one another to be the best person they can be and to help one another grow stronger in God.

A good husband serves as a guide for the rest of the family; he sets the example for the way a man should care for his wife and children, and he carries himself as the man of integrity when he's in the public eye. He maintains a legitimate source of income and he brings his entire revenue home to share with his family. A good wife is an accountant in her own right; she takes care of the home; she knows (for example) when the refrigerator is empty, when the children are sick or need new things, when something in the house needs repairs, etc., so she is given the power and authority to delegate where the family's money is distributed. The children obey their mother and their father, and they take heed to the lessons being taught, as these are life lessons that are designed to prepare them for the real world!

The love and fellowship you share within your household will be the motivation for your family to stay happy, healthy, and prosperous. Take a genuine interest in your family member's hobbies and interests; be the first to show them that you care and that you support their endeavors. Give feedback on how they can improve what may seem to be a good idea, and help them make it into something great! Offer a shoulder to cry on or an ear to express their feelings when you see your loved ones in want/need of attention. When love can be found inside of the home, you reduce the need or desire to outsource.

Friendship is the key to romance, and its romance that brought you the relationship that you're currently in. A husband should be a wife's best male friend, and a wife should be a husband's best female friend; value this union and let no one come between it. Many will try to break the sanctity of your union, but know that for the "outsider", this challenge is merely for sport. They have no real desire to build a relationship of substance with you. They simply want to see how close they can get to you and to prove that by you giving your time/energy/effort to them, you can't possibly be as happy and/or exclusive as you *claim* to be. Let *no one* break your family's bond!

Being single gives us a great deal of independence; a feeling that for a long time we are reluctant to give up. And for this reason I say, relationships and marriages aren't for everybody; relationships and marriages are only for the ready! Committing to a relationship means that you are willing to *share* your world with someone else. If you're sharing your world with someone and they're sharing their world with you… your independence then becomes "interdependence". You're not giving up your independence; you're merely coming together with someone who is also independent and *doubling* your resources. If you have nothing to give and/or if you're not willing to share your world, you are not ready to be in a relationship/marriage.

Sometimes when you're single, you and your friends may lose all sense of time. When you're in a relationship or marriage, *timing* is of the essence. When you're single and independent, there's no one that you have to consider. When you have a family, there's *everyone* in your home to consider. When you're by yourself, you can afford to miss a meal. When you're accountable for others you have to make sure *everyone* gets fed.

The same people you spend your leisure time with while you're *away* from your family should be welcome in your home *amongst* your family. If your significant other has a problem with the company you keep, then you should prioritize and determine which relationship means the most to you. Surround yourself with happy, healthy, and prosperous people, and invite those same individuals to fellowship with the people who are important in your life (i.e. your family). The people whom you associate with the most on a personal level have the capacity to influence your behavior and your decisions, so choose wisely. Sometimes starting a new life will require new friends.

If you come to realize that you're not ready for a relationship and/or marriage, take the noble pursuit by being honest with yourself and your partner about it. Commit to someone if/when you can afford to give a part of yourself to another. Having children with someone binds you for life; however it doesn't necessarily contract the two of you in a lifelong *romantic* relationship with one another. If your relationship with your partner doesn't work out, the two of you should continue to treat one another with dignity and respect for the sake of the child and for peace of mind. While separated, take time to focus on yourself, your child, and your future. Keep the family together in spirit.

Being responsible means that you have something to lose and that you're not willing to lose it.

Food, Sex & Peace of Mind

Be *responsible* for your family! If you lose your family, you may come to find that your *family members* were the only ones who *really* wanted you around and loved you unconditionally. There is nothing more important than family! Not work, not sex, not money, and certainly not things! There is nothing more valuable than your family's fellowship. Make the people you love and the people you care about number one in your life.

Chapter Six

Understanding A Man

All Men Have A Motive

Males and females are built differently, they *think* differently, and they *act* differently. It's because of this fact that it's extremely important that you *know* your audience. When it comes to relationships, the same things you would normally say or do in front of a *female* audience would have to be fine-tuned to fit a *male* audience. For example, your female friends might be totally fine with talking on the phone, going to lunch, and even spending the night over each other's house without any ulterior motives. Your male friends however would use talking on the phone, going to lunch, and spending the night over each other's houses as a way to get closer to you romantically. Knowing your audience and governing yourself accordingly will help you avoid a world of ambiguous situations when dealing with men.

If you're in a relationship or marriage, your *partner* should be your one and only best friend of the opposite sex. He's invested the time, energy, effort, and money and quite frankly he's *earned* exclusive access to you. Since he's proven himself worthy of your commitment, he's more than deserving of your loyalty and devotion. It's a great idea to introduce your partner to any friends you might have early on in the relationship, however *certain* acquaintances should never be introduced or even mentioned, and those are the ones whom you know are romantically interested in you.

A man introduces himself to a woman based on his sexual attraction to her, and in many cases, before he's able to succeed in sleeping with her, he finds himself in the *friendship zone*. No matter how long a

152

man is kept in the friendship zone, his main objective is to figure out a way to get out. If you'll notice, a man's "female friends" are always beautiful, and that's not by coincidence, it's by *design*! His reasoning for choosing a beautiful woman as a friend is because he ultimately wants to sleep with her, and in most cases *friendship* is the title *she* gives him. Men who are romantically interested in you will not *stop* being romantically interested in you just because you're now in a relationship or marriage.

When a man is romantically interested in you, he's looking to establish a *mutually* beneficial arrangement. What this means is, he's willing to do things for you in hopes that you'd be also willing to do things for him. Anytime he shows you favor, he'll be keeping a tab and patiently waiting to collect. Everyone knows that the fastest way to make a woman run away is by telling her that you want sex, so a "Plan B" would be to use friendship as a subtle approach to getting closer to you romantically. You may feel as though *you're* able to maintain a platonic friendship, but that's not the issue.

The issue is that this person you call a "friend" knows intricate details about your life, he has exclusive access to you, he knows your points of vulnerability, and *that's* what makes your man feel uncomfortable. A person who's that close to you, knows that much about you, and has that deep of a connection with you should *be* your man. If your best friend isn't your boyfriend, he should be promoted. If your boyfriend isn't your best friend, he should be demoted! There can only be one king of the castle, and no other man should feel even remotely as close in significance as the main man in your life.

If a man outside of your relationship needs a woman to confide in, he should turn to *his* woman or his mother for that kind of support. The same applies to *you* when you need a man to confide in; you don't turn to a man outside of your relationship for support, you turn to the man who's in your life, or your father for these benefits. You will quickly come to find that you are *not* welcome in another man's life when he's in a relationship, because his woman won't want you to have exclusive access to *her* man… and rightfully so! This is the value of being in an *exclusive* relationship with someone; you gain *exclusive* rights and privileges that no one else has. The men on the outside looking in had their opportunity to become exclusive and since they didn't put forth the time, energy, effort, and money to seal the deal, they shouldn't be granted any exclusive access or privileges.

Whoever you choose to be significant in your life should be someone you can also call your *best friend.* He should be someone who is *more* than a lover, *more* than a protector, and *more* than a provider so that you won't need to outsource to another man for what he's lacking. This is why that special someone is referred to as "The One"! He's that individual who offers everything you look for in a man and *more*!

When you've found the one, you then refer to any and all of the other men in your life as *acquaintances*, giving them *less* significance than that of your partner. Sure, be grateful for all the men who have always been there for you, but know that those men were "there" (as a friend) because of their desire to be *more*! Since you're in a committed monogamous relationship now, these male friends need to understand that things *change* when your relationship status changes. The things that were acceptable while you were single are no longer acceptable when you're in a relationship or marriage.

No matter your relationship status, a male admirer will always be ready and willing to sleep with you. In fact, it's more convenient for him to sleep with you with no strings when you're in a relationship because he knows you won't want to pursue anything further. And furthermore, he wouldn't consider you for anything more than sex anyway, because you've proven to be someone who isn't loyal and cannot be trusted. This understanding between two adults can make for the perfect recipe for infidelity if the right opportunity presented itself. The best way to avoid temptation is simply to avoid temptation. The more time you spend with a person, the deeper the connection becomes, and the greater the chances of you lusting over one another.

By removing yourself from these situations, you lessen the chances of you being propositioned and/or being violated. By placing yourself in these situations, you portray a sense of naivety and even rebellion towards what your man might consider to be *danger*, and this gesture may lose his trust. Life is about building relationships and leaving behind legacies. When you commit to someone, focus on your Plan A, not your Plan B. Your Plan A should be, learning more about your partner, growing with him, and figuring out ways to add value to one another's lives. Anyone on the outside of your relationship should come second to what you're trying to build upon, and the ones lucky enough to be in your circle should be the *help*, not the *hurt.*

It's perfectly natural for a man to be *territorial* and want exclusive access to his woman. After all, this is the exact same respect you would want from him. A man knows how other men maneuver, and he knows all of the techniques men use to get closer to a woman. He wants to feel secure in knowing that not only is his woman smart enough to identify with this approach, but also that she respects him enough not to entertain such relationships with other men, whether she's mutually interested in them or not. Your man may very well trust *you*, but it's the other *men* he doesn't trust, and rightfully so.

When a straight man is ok with being "just friends" with a female, he either has already had sex with her, is currently having sex with her, or he wants to have sex with her and is simply waiting for her to be vulnerable. For the men on the outside, being a "friend" is one of the *best* places to be when a woman is going through something in her relationship or marriage. She looks at him like a "brother", she trusts him, and doesn't think he'll ever cross any lines (because he knows you're in a relationship or marriage). Truth be told… he doesn't look at you like a sister; never has, and never will! He will sleep with you the first opportunity you give him (no matter what *your* relationship status is, and no matter what *his* relationship status is).

With the exception of family, any straight man that remains affiliated with you (whether he makes it clear or not) is interested in sleeping with you. When you're in a relationship with someone, your relationship with other men should cease and desist.

Learn How To Speak "Man"

Men and women are and always will be *different.* The beauty of being a woman is that you're granted *special* privileges, and you don't have to work *as* hard to get the things you want. A lot of women haven't yet realized or taken advantage of their true power because they're busy taking on the responsibility of a man instead of enjoying the fruits of being a woman. Yes, it's *essential* that a woman establishes her independence when she's on her own, but it's equally important that a woman learn how to be *interdependent* when there's a man in her life. What this means is… *Enjoy being a woman*! Men *love* doing nice things for a woman; all he needs is the motivation to do so. When it comes to men and relationships, motivation is *anything* that inspires him to keep you around.

It's important for you to know that men and women don't always value the same things, we're not always treated the same way, and many of the things we experience in life are in part *because* of the gender we were born. From the very moment a mother and a father come to know a child's gender, they begin to speculate on how they plan on interacting with the child in the future. It's because of this gender specific treatment; a male and a female are likely to respond differently to many of life's challenges, especially when it comes to relationships. But it's ok for men and woman to be different; in fact, that's what makes being *together* all the more unique! You *share* your differences and introduce one another to different perspectives pertaining to *Life*. One of the best ways to grow is through learning from *others*.

If you're associating yourself with people who

don't add value to your life, or who don't provide you with *meaningful* new insight, your time together will prove to be counter-productive. On the other hand, if you associate yourself with someone who thinks differently, challenges you, and has a mind of their own, etc., you'll open yourself to potentially learning *new* things. What you do with the information is totally up to you, but you'll at least have an additional *valuable* perspective to add to your own.

This is why guys can't hang out with guys *all* the time and girls can't hang out with girls *all* the time. Over time, you'll begin to feel *smothered* and want to be exposed to something *different*. The same is true when you're in a relationship, you'll need an *escape* from one another, and a healthy, positive escape from your partner would be your friends of the same sex. It's a great idea to have that *balance* in your life, because too much of one thing is never a good thing. If your partner doesn't have any friends of their own, this may cause a problem because you'll be their *only* source of entertainment. Always pay close attention to your significant other's resources, so that they won't self-sabotage the relationship with their clinginess/neediness.

No matter who a man is, where he's from, or how much money he has, what men value the most is *Peace of mind!* When a man is in a relationship with a woman who offers him peace of mind, he is more than happy to come home to her. When a man does not have a woman at home that offers him peace of mind, he'll find any and every excuse to make home the *last* place he returns to, because unfortunately, *home* (for him) isn't the happiest place on earth. If you want your man to be motivated to be in a relationship with you, and motivated to come home to you, one of the key ingredients you will need is offering him *peace of mind.*

There will be times where you're faced with a dilemma that you want your man to pay special attention to, and you're not sure how to approach him for the best possible results. Always keep in mind that men are *used to* facing and dealing with problems, so don't worry yourself with the details of the problem, just gently bring it to his attention, and trust that he'll be able to fix it! When a man is faced with a problem, his first priority is figuring out *how to* fix it. Dwelling on the issue isn't of any value to a man because it doesn't make the problem go away; when a man is faced with a problem, he simply wants it to *go away*! If you come to your man and let him know exactly what the problem is, and even offer a little insight on what he can do to fix it, you will come to find that he is more than happy to do whatever it takes to put you at ease, and bring peace of mind back into the relationship.

If on the other hand your approach is startling, defensive, aggravating, or just plain annoying, a man will naturally be on the defense, which will prolong the "problem solving process". When a man is *approached* with aggression, he *responds* with aggression. In other words, if it's a fight you're looking for, a fight is exactly what you're going to get! But if you're looking to find a solution to a problem, start by making sure he's in a peaceful place, and in a calm mood, so that he can listen to your problem, and be mentally prepared to quickly and effectively find a solution.

Once the problem is fixed, it no longer matters (to him) how it happened. You can't change the past, but you can look forward to the future. In other words, the end justifies the means; allow him to do what he does best by giving him a task and allowing him to complete it. Men care more about fixing the problem, than the *actual* problem itself, whereas a woman sometimes needs to express her thoughts and feelings on the problem itself. With women, talking about the problem itself could last for hours, days, weeks, months, and even years, but as mentioned earlier, men want and *need* peace in his home and in his relationship.

Arguing about *anything* is nerve-racking and will always make a man question why he's in a relationship, as opposed to simply being single. I'm annoyed just thinking and writing about arguing with a woman (lol). When a man is single, he's not obligated to listen, respond, or care about a woman's feelings, so don't tempt him! A relationship should *add* value to a person's life, not take it away, so when a man opts to be in a relationship with you, give him reassurance that the relationship you have is *more* beneficial than the single life. No relationship is perfect, but no relationship should be unbearable to the point where he no longer sees the value in being committed to you.

Being in a relationship is a beautiful thing, however having a life outside of one another can offer that *balance* you need in order to stay sane. This is why a man finds so much joy in being with his boys! There are no chores, no emotionally charged conversations that could lead to a break up, no whining or crying, and no clinging to one another. You can apply these very same principles to your relationship, in hopes to keep your man satisfied. Be "one of the boys" in the sense that you're fun to be around, easy to talk to, and don't want any drama, but be his *woman* when it comes to romance.

Another very important thing women need to know about men is… men like *simplicity*. The moment a woman complicates things, he will begin to question whether or not he still wants to be committed to her. A man likes to do *nothing* until it's time to do *something*. He can sit around, watch TV, eat, sleep and do absolutely nothing all day long and be A-Okay with doing so! A woman who will allow him to sit there and enjoy doing what he loves to do will have a much greater chance at remaining that special woman in his life. It's a relationship, so of course he can't sit around doing nothing *all* the time, but because you've granted him this freedom, and this liberty, he will *then* be motivated to reward you for being so understanding.

A man who is of substance and is in a relationship for true love will do *anything* for his woman. A great way to measure whether or not you're dealing with a man of substance is by his willingness to do things for you. A man who isn't genuinely interested in being with you will have a problem with just about *any* request you make (i.e. fixing a light bulb, changing a tire, or simply running an errand for you). A man who loves will tell you "Ok babe, I'll do it in a minute"! A man who loves you will always be willing to do what you've asked of him, simply because it will bring peace to the relationship. When a man of substance finds you, do all that is in your power to keep him!

What A Man Needs From His Woman!

Food, Sex & Peace of Mind is what a woman needs to know to keep a man! It sounds simple, and it is, however a more strategic approach needs to be taken in order to make this attempt at keeping him happy, *successful*! A man always knows what he wants from a woman, but he sometimes needs a little help with seeing the value in what he truly needs! When you connect with a man, your advantage over other women will come based on the value you add to his life (outside of the bedroom). Getting to know a man on the inside and out will be your playbook for figuring out how to play offense, win him over, and in the end get him to celebrate you! The quality of your giving will make all the difference in the quality of your relationship.

If you leave it up to a man, he will be A-ok with the simple things in life, the bare minimum, or stuck in his "whatever works" mentality. Everything is black and white when it comes to men, and this is where the value of a woman comes into play; a woman adds vibrancy, color, and an abundance of love into the picture. He may be ok with eating *Ramen Noodles* for dinner 7 nights a week, but he would much rather have a home cooked meal prepared by a loving, caring woman. He will immediately see the value in having you around, and he will want to hold onto you because of that value, which would've been otherwise missed had you sat back and watched him eat Ramen Noodles every night. There's nothing wrong with Ramen Noodles (I personally love them), but anytime there's an opportunity for you to upgrade your man, it's in your best interest to make an *attempt* to take it!

162

What A Man Needs From His Woman!

Many women today are convinced that men do not want to be in long-term monogamous relationships, and that couldn't be further from the truth. A man simply wants to reach certain milestones in his life before taking on the responsibility that comes along with a commitment. In other words, he doesn't *yet* feel as though he is worthy, and he's doing the honorable thing by sparing you the heartache, pain, and struggle of being in a relationship with a man who's simply not *ready*. When a man is finally ready spiritually, emotionally, and financially, he's in his *Single By Design* mode, and he's not looking to settle for just *anyone*! When a man achieves greatness, he will be looking to commit to a great woman.

A man knows the role he wants a woman to play in his life before he even meets her. This is why it's important for you as a woman, to know who you are and show who you are so that when you come across a man who's finally ready to settle down, he will immediately see value in you, and consider you for a future. He's looking for an upgrade! Someone who can take his life, relationship, business, and family to the next level, as opposed to simply keeping him leveled. Men are simple and like to do simple things, but on his own time, and his own way! Although he may want less, being with a woman will guarantee that he gets more, because at some point or another, a woman eventually wants *more*.

Healthy relationships never stop growing; in order for a relationship to successfully grow, you have to continually plant new seeds, love and nurture it, and watch everything that you've invested come into fruition. If you come into a relationship with the same exact values as a man (i.e. eating Ramen Noodles 7 nights a week), at some point or another, he's going to say to himself "Why am I with her? I can eat Ramen Noodles, sit around and watch TV, etc with my boys or by myself and spend less. Where's the value in this relationship? Sure, the sex is great, but we're not growing! She's just "here"!" Don't let this scenario be you; take a man's simplicity and upgrade him with your creativity!

If you want your relationship to be a success, you have to work towards making it a success! The goals you put in place for yourself as an individual and for each other as a couple will give you something to look forward to each and everyday. If you grow complacent, your relationship will get stale, and one or both parties will seek something and/or someone that is worth looking forward to. In efforts to work towards relationship success, keep in mind "The 7 Habits of Highly Effective Relationships (According to CheyB). Respect, Love, Trust, Loyalty, Honesty, Support, and Communication.

Respect: There is no limit to how far a man will go for you if he believes in his heart that you are someone who respects who he is and all that he does. Each and every one of us seeks validation from someone else on one level or another; for a man, he takes pride in knowing that he is able to be of value to his woman. Everything you say and do will show just how much you love and respect your significant other, or the lack thereof. His motivation to do better and be better will come through the person he values the most! If you are in his life, your respect isn't just wanted, but it's needed in order for him to feel confident about the future of your relationship.

Love: A man's home is his place of peace; it's where he rejuvenates his mind, body, and spirit! A man will involve you in everything if you are being his everything! (i.e. Lover, fighter, cook, accountant, adviser, masseuse, you name it). A relationship is about creating "win wins" for both parties; you are a team, you stick together, and you continually add value to each other's lives. If you find that your man is in a bad mood, you have to remember that the two of you are *one*, or working towards becoming one, so use this opportunity to remind him of why *you* are the most important woman in his life. Continue to show him love, appreciation, and affection so that he'll never have a reason to treat you with anything less.

Trust: There is power in words, so speak them into existence, but do so with an open and honest heart! When using your words, follow through with your actions, and make sure that they are both in alignment; this will build your significant other's confidence in you and will also strengthen the bond in your relationship. When building trust, do so out of selflessness, not selfishness; you want to keep secrets *with* your partner, not *from* your partner. Being true to yourself starts with loving yourself; when love is present, it's evident, and needs no explanation. When love is absent, in comes cloudy vision, lies, deceit, cover ups, etc, which in turn raises your significant other's awareness. People who have taken the time to truly love themselves know what *true* love looks and feels like, so don't allow selfishness to ruin what could potentially be a winning team. Stay true to him, as you would want him to stay true to you.

Loyalty Be consistent with your character and remember that you both are on the same team and are playing to win! When your significant other is not around, he should feel confident in knowing that you are treating yourself with the same dignity and respect as you would if he were standing right next to you. The slightest bit of betrayal can bruise a man's ego, and hurt his pride, which will cause turmoil in your relationship. A man wants to know that he is number one in your life, and that no other man or woman (outside of your family) gets the privilege of having a *number* in your book. Your loyalty to one another is one of the most important things that will keep you together!

Honesty: Life is about building relationships and leaving behind legacies. When it comes to the growth and development of your relationship, let go of the past, and look forward to your future. If you want your significant other to love who you are, he needs to know who you are. Being transparent will allow your partner to see your strengths, your weaknesses and everything else in between. When you allow your partner to see who you are, where you are strong, and where you are weak, you then allow him to see which areas he will be able to help you the most. That moment of vulnerability could mean a lifetime of victory!

Support: If your man is struggling financially, be his cheerleader, his motivation, his inspiration, and his support system as he works towards getting back on his feet. Instead of being the woman who holds him down, be the woman who lifts him up! It's easy to to commit to someone when everything is good, but the real challenge will come when everything is bad! The way you handle yourself, your partner, and your relationship under turbulent times will confirm where you stand as an individual, and as a couple, and will have a great impact on your relationship's future.

Submission is also a very powerful tool that will only grant you more and more of your man's favor. When you submit, you're showing him that you want him to lead, and that you trust and respect his judgment/leadership. A man has his pride, and pride can be quite useful when it's focused in areas that inspire growth! If for example, a man is proud to be a servant of God, loyal husband, father, and contributor in his community, that's a beautiful thing, and as his woman, you should be proud as well. When a man is proud of something, or passionate about something, be there to support him, or be there to advise him on how to upgrade his ideas, vision, and/or passion.

Communication: With wisdom comes understanding! Men and women communicate differently, and that's ok because this will challenge you to adapt in unfamiliar territory. Once you understand the way men prefer to send and receive messages, you will find it much easier to get what you want and with a great attitude (on his part). Men are simple, so don't make things complicated; if you want something done, simply let him know what it is you want, and leave him to it! If you have additional information that might be helpful, by all means share it, and then (again), leave him to it. He will figure it out in his own way and on his own time, but rest assured, he *will* figure out. The best part is, you will get what you want (minus the fuss) and in the end, everyone's happy!

What a man needs in his life is a woman who has wisdom; someone who understands him and accepts him for who he is as opposed to trying to mold him into someone she wants him to be. A woman who is a great listener, communicator (not to be confused with speaker), supporter, who can be his go-to girl for everything he needs. As his woman, it's in your best interest to be innovative and have the ability to adjust, figure things out, and accommodate him. If he has everything he needs at home, he'll have no reason to outsource.

A Man Knows If You're The One From Day One

Before a man even approaches a woman, he knows exactly which role he wants that woman to play in his life. With each and every woman that he meets, he looks for ways she can *add* value to his life. With this in mind, it's essential that you always put your best foot forward because the introduction is everything! The image that you present sets the tone for the *value* he places on you. From the very first moment he lays eyes on you, you will be categorized as one or more of the following: 1) A potential wife 2) A potential sex slave 3) A potential resource.

It's true that a man will categorize a woman based on her presentation and treat her according to the category he placed her in, but in addition to that, what prompts him to entertain any one of these types of women is the way he feels about *himself*. The way he feels about himself is always subject to change, but is primarily inspired by his spiritual, emotional, and financial position. The best way to evaluate whether or not a man is emotionally, spiritually, or financially stable is by simply taking the time to get to know him *prior* to sleeping with him. Once you've slept with him, you'll have already made yourself vulnerable to him emotionally, and will tend to overlook his shortcomings as a result.

SIDE NOTE:- Your vagina is your negotiating power! Once you give it up, you are no longer in a position to negotiate. Get all you want and need out of a man *before* sleeping with him (i.e. A ring).

When a man is not financially stable, he won't be ready, willing, or able to pursue a relationship or a marriage. At this point in his life, he can't afford a commitment, and it'd be more beneficial for him to pursue a woman who offers sex and resources. When a man is not emotionally available, he won't allow a woman to get close to his heart, but he'll gladly let a woman get close to his body as it will take his mind off of his problems. In this case, he will seek out the woman who offers *sex*! When a man is not spiritually grounded, there's a chance he will choose any of the three options, however, the quality of those relationships will always be at risk because he has no *principle based* focus.

Each and every woman has an opportunity to show the world who they are, and the choices they make will determine who will choose to associate with them or the lack thereof. Many people make decisions that reflect their character but are ignorant to the fact that what they did or what they said *does* in fact portray *who they are* to the world! We've all gone to the mall, tried on clothes, and looked at ourselves in the mirror saying "This is ME!" Well when you wear those provocative outfits anywhere out in public, you're saying to the world "This is ME!" So before a man has the opportunity to even walk up to you and say hello, he already has an idea of who you are, and will categorize you accordingly.

If a man decides to approach this provocatively dressed woman, he automatically knows that at the very least, he wants to have her as his sex slave. A sex slave is the value that he feels she can/will add to his life based on the way she presented herself. He'll assume that because she's dressed this way that her esteem is low, and she's looking for attention. A man who's not financially stable, emotionally unavailable, or spiritually grounded doesn't have to invest anything more than time & energy into *this* type of woman, because in many cases, that's all she requires.

If for example a man is struggling financially, or has been hurt, abandoned, or disappointed by a woman in his past relationship(s), it will cause him to close his heart off to the possibility of love. When a man is on the prowl looking for a woman in this state of mind, he will settle for the ones who in some way shape or form embody these very same characteristics. It's an unhealthy solution to his problem, but it's a road that many men take just to help them get by. You don't want to find yourself caught up with a man who has this state of mind, because his misery can rub off on you.

It takes a man quite some time to become spiritually grounded, financially stable, and emotionally available, but when he does, he's more likely to search for a woman using his *heart*. What this means is he'll be motivated to pursue a woman not only based on her *outer* beauty, but also based on her *inner* beauty. A woman can show her inner beauty by being selfless, showing kindness to others, and by giving off positive vibes. When a man is looking for a relationship of substance, he will want to pursue a woman who embodies the qualities of a wife, and will overlook anything less for this position.

Women who show they have low self-esteem make easy targets for men who aren't at their best. What's worst is, since a man categorizes you before he meets you, he will limit how close you can get to his heart. No matter how many years you've been dealing with each other, or how much you've been through, it's the *introduction* that's making him act so cold and never warming up to you. He didn't respect you *or* himself when he accepted you into his life, and if you're still in his life, he'll resent the fact that he *still* hasn't outgrown you. Your purpose in his life was never to walk down the aisle; this was decided before he even met you! Your purpose in his life was dependent on the way you first presented yourself, and on the current position he was in when he met you.

Sometimes a woman may have *access* to something that a man needs, and he may see *you* as an opportunity to get closer to the *real* prize. If he's unable to go directly for the gold, he'll reach the gold through *you!* He'll play whatever part he needs to play in order to keep the resources coming, however your purpose in his life was never to be more than just a resource. No matter how much you do for him, or how good you are to him, he has already placed you in a category that works for him, and has no intention of letting you out. What you want and need from a relationship is a man who's with you for *love*, and can appreciate the extra-added bonuses that come along with an open, honest, loving, and caring relationship.

Any and everything you do, from the car you buy, to the dress you wear, to the words you speak is a reflection of your character. When a man looks for a woman, he's the equivalent of a casting director. He's looking for characters that fit the role for the leading lady in his life! Always present yourself as the person you want to be known and remembered as. Carry yourself with dignity and integrity no matter where you

172

go, or who you feel is watching, because people (especially men) are always watching. You won't always be given a second chance to show a man who you are, so take full advantage of the first opportunity you get and make a great, long-lasting impression.

Physical beauty will certainly *get* a man's attention, but it certainly will not *keep* a man's attention. If lord forbid something were to happen to your physical appearance or ability to produce sexual stimulation, you may find yourself abandoned by the man you *thought* pursued you for love. From the very beginning though, he's already made up in his mind that *this* woman is simply someone he'd like to have as a sex slave and nothing more. When a man determines that you're worth less, he'll never treat you like you're worth more. He instead will utilize you for what he *does* in fact feel you are worth (sex).

When a man comes across a woman he feels is *The One*, he will do everything in his power to both get *and* keep her. He'll be open and willing to take a chance on love not only because of the way she looks, but also because of the way she makes him feel. There will be no doubt in his mind that she's the one for him; in fact, any doubts about her being "The One" will only be put in place by "her" actions throughout the relationship. Choosing the right woman will be dependent on both the woman's presentation, and the position he is currently in financially, emotionally & spiritually. So ladies, half the battle is the man being ready, the other half is making sure *you* are presenting yourself as someone who's ready. Always present yourself as the person you want to be known and remembered as.

The Reason He Won't Invite You Out

There are quite a few factors that come into play when it comes to the way a man will treat you. Some of the reasons are is his upbringing, his male influences, and the morals, values, and principles he's grown accustomed to. Another major factor would be his current position in life (i.e. His living situation, his financial situation, and his self-esteem). And lastly, the way he feels about *you*. The way he feels about you will be determined solely on what he knows about you and your character.

What he knows about you is concluded based on what you've shown him during the introduction (i.e. where you both met, what you were wearing, the words that were exchanged, etc.). If during the introduction you came off (to him) as an honorable & respectable woman, he will do one of three things a) Treat you with dignity and respect and attempt forming a relationship with you b) Leave you alone because he's not at a place in his life where he can match up to or appreciate you b) Turn on his charm and attempt to entertain you for as long as he's able to keep up!

It's extremely important for you to know how the man who's interested in you *truly* feels about you. It's equally important to know how he truly feels about *himself* and his current position in life. If this is someone you're considering for a relationship, don't be afraid to ask him questions regarding his life, just do so in a subtle manner. If he doesn't love himself, there's no way he could possibly love you. Also, if he's unable to take care of himself financially and emotionally, there's no way he could take care of a woman, and there's no way he could take care of a child, if sex &

pregnancy were to come into the picture.

You can't control who you fall in love with because love is *unpredictable*. Love though is only *one* factor to consider when it comes to your relationship. When you come across a man who is not financially, emotionally, or spiritually stable, and you *really* want to see him do better for himself, the best approach is to remove yourself (as a love interest) and be there for him (as a friend). Not only will he respect you more for being such a supportive woman in his life, you'll help him become the *best* man he can be. A man can love, protect, and provide for you *much* better once he's at his best. If you see no potential in this man, there's no value in continuing to associate because there's no room for growth.

Friendship is the key to romance, so if you're able to develop a strong bond with him prior to a romantic relationship, he will view sex as an *added* bonus to the substance you already offer him. While he's establishing himself, you're not *waiting* for him to be the best man (for you); you're continuing to live your life and hoping for the best for him. If another relationship comes along, by all means go for it. If by the time the other guy gets his life together, and you're available, feel free to pursue it. It's essential never to commit to *potential*; instead commit to a man once he's reached his potential.

Lack of financial stability will be *one* of the reasons why a man you're mutually interested in might not take you out. In some cases, it's not because he doesn't *want* to take you out, but merely because he can't afford to. And if he can't afford to, his priority will be and certainly needs to be *finding* financial stability, and *keeping* it so that he can provide for himself, enjoy life's pleasures, and potentially be an asset to a woman's life (if he plans on pursuing dating/relationships).

The other instance where a man might not invite you out is if he feels you're not worth it. If he views you as just someone he can sleep with, the chances are he will not want to spend a dime on you, but he will do *everything* in his power to try to get you in bed. A date (for him) would be a very last resort because he views a date as an *investment*! An investment is something he would rather use towards a woman he's genuinely interested in pursuing for a relationship. If you're sexually attractive enough and the bare minimum hasn't gotten him sex, it's possible that he will use a date or two to speed up the process.

This is why the presentation is so important, because it sets the tone for future conversations, dating, and the overall relationship. Once he's categorized you as non-potential, there's no changing his mind. Everyone has their own taste, and their own values, so it doesn't matter how beautiful you are, how long your list of credentials are, what type of treatment you're used to, because not every man values the same qualities as the last or the next. If you want a man to know your worth, you have to show your worth. You won't have a 2nd opportunity to convince him of who you are, because he's already analyzed you based on your level of integrity. Your integrity reflects the things you do and the things you say when you're unaware that you're being watched.

There are quite a few ways to measure whether or not a man is truly interested in you. Men value their time and their money, so if you can somehow get him to part with either one or both, that's a great sign that he might be interested in you. A man doesn't like to be led (especially when he's broke or not interested), so tread lightly when inviting a man out to events and such. A safe way to get a man to part with his time or his money is to politely ask when you can see each other. With this approach, you're not inviting him anywhere, nor are you making any suggestions, but you're opening up a door for possibilities. From there, you can sit back, relax and enjoy being a woman!

Once you let a man know you'd like to see him, it's now up to *him* to make a suggestion on where to go, when to go, and what to do. Use the suggestion that he makes to measure either his financial situation, or the way he feels about *you*. Not every man you meet is going to be your knight in shining armor, nor is every man going to be marriage material. Do your best to evaluate each man's position, and throw *him* in a category of your own. Knowing is *half* the battle; if you know a man is broke, doesn't love you, or doesn't have your best interest at heart, you now have the information you need to plan your next move.

Life is short, it's beautiful, and everyone living it ultimately is on his or her own spiritual journey to pursue happiness. Not every man you're attracted to is guaranteed to be at the peak of his career, in the best emotional state, or have made a connection with a higher power. A vast majority of what a man does in life is *for* a woman, so having a woman in his life can very well be *the* motivation he needs to do and *be* better. When you meet individuals who have potential, but haven't reached it, you can use this as an opportunity to show him the true meaning of *friendship*.

Friendship is one of the most critical factors in any relationships, and it's highly overlooked by many. Often times a man is at his most humble and most vulnerable state when he's hit rock bottom, and all he needs is a *friend* to help him reach his potential. Even if a romantic relationship doesn't transpire initially, the two of you will have developed a solid friendship that you can stand on. If a man is truly interested in you, and is not financially stable, you'll notice that he will *still* make an effort to do *something* for you, and who knows… that *something* might be the best dating experience you've ever had, even from men who "have it all".

When a man is not genuinely interested in you, *seeing* you won't be a priority in his life, but more so a *convenience*. Under these circumstances, any meeting between the two of you will have to be on *his* terms; otherwise he'll be reluctant to extend himself. Any suggestion to go anywhere or do anything with *him* will result in a recommendation of something of lesser value (i.e. a trip to a hotel or his bedroom). A simple walk in the park might even seem troublesome to him because it requires *time* and attention. The less effort he's willing to put forth in entertaining you, the less he's genuinely interested in you.

There are millions of men in this world and you only need *one.* Men are always on the prowl in search of women for many different purposes; the good news is *you* can influence *why* men approach you. A hunter doesn't hunt aimlessly; he targets his prey based on his personal desire, his strengths, and on the quality of the capture. If you want to attract a man who is of

178

substance, knows how to be gentlemen, and is looking for a woman of substance, then continue to present yourself as a lady and associate with like minds. You don't have to look for a man or a relationship, but always be ready for one! A man has to find *himself* before finding a woman. He knows where to find a good woman, and he'll look in that direction when he's ready.

A Man Can Only Love One Woman At A Time

When two people connect with one another romantically, there's a *hint* of love being shared (if nothing else). Depending on the relationship, this love can either be short-term, or long-term. Although men have been trained from childhood to be strong, tough, and hide the way he's truly feeling, women have proven to be very successful at bringing these guards down. A man loves the idea of opening up and expressing himself openly and freely, but he only does this with people he knows, trusts, and has developed a spiritual connection with. Prior to this spiritual connection, a man will only allow a woman access to him externally, while he guards himself internally.

Once a man finds a woman he can be himself with, he'll fall deeply in love, and will share his thoughts, his dreams, and even his life's stories with her. If allowed, he will share himself with her sexually, however what keeps him coming back is the *substance* offered in the relationship. He finds joy and happiness in being with a woman who can offer more than just a rump in the hay, but even though he's happy, it doesn't necessarily mean he won't go astray. *Loyalty* from a man is one thing a woman has no control over; loyalty is something that's instilled in a man's character from his early stages of childhood, so thoroughly get to know a man and his past to get an idea of his level of loyalty. Anytime a man steps outside of the relationship, it's not because he's in love with another woman, or that he doesn't love you, it's simply because he doesn't see the value in *commitment*.

A Man Can Only Love One Woman At A Time

The woman on the side is merely a source of entertainment, and after he's done with her, he plans on going back home to where his heart is (his *safety net*). Men with poor morals and values sometimes allow their body's to drift to another woman's bed, while his heart remains with the woman he has at home. He doesn't allow the woman on the side to get too close to his heart because he reserves this exclusive access only for *his* main woman. Even though there are two women in the picture, he'll always *love* one, and strictly *lust* the other. A man of substance and integrity seeks a spiritual & physical connection solely from the one woman he loves and holds dear.

Disclaimer: No matter the reasoning, cheating is a selfish act, it's unacceptable, and should never be tolerated in any relationship.

When people commit to a romantic relationship, they share precious details and aspects of their lives (i.e. family, history, intimacy, etc.). In order for a man to get this deeply involved with a woman, it will require extreme vulnerability; being vulnerable is much easier to do once a man finds himself and reaches a level of contentment (spiritually, emotionally, and financially). When a man of substance is *in* love with a woman, his values shift; he honors and appreciates the woman he has at home and will let nothing come between them. It's when a man does not truly value himself or the relationship that he's open and willing to share himself with another woman. When you notice that a man doesn't value his mind, body, soul, and even his money, you can't allow yourself to submit to him and/or give

Food, Sex & Peace of Mind

him a position in your life.

Relationships aren't for everybody; relationships are only for the ready! When a man is truly ready to be in a relationship, he'll have reached a point in his life where he wants to have something *exclusive*. A vast majority of men don't reach this point in their lives until they've had their fair share of encounters with multiple different women. No matter how long it takes for a man you like to find himself, you should use this time focusing on "you", not him! Being single has its perks, but one of the things that's always missing is *exclusivity*; knowing who, when, where, and why you're sleeping with someone.

Not every man is mature enough to admit that he's not ready for a relationship, and *some* men will even commit to a woman just to keep her around. All the while, he'll have multiple different women that he entertains on the side. One might ask, "Why would a man do this as opposed to simply being single and living his life?" It's because he's selfish, but more importantly, he's *lost*! He loves the idea of companionship, family life, exclusivity, but he can't let go of the mistresses, the lies, and the deceit. He needs to take a step back from relationships and find himself before he finds a woman.

Love is something that a man learns how to do primarily from a woman! *Survival* is something that a man learns how to do primarily from another man. When a man entertains multiple women, he's not doing it out of *love*; he's doing it as a way to *survive*! He's trying to find his way, and while doing so, he stops to indulge himself in the warm, loving, caring environment(s) that a woman offers. He's not *in* love with any of these women; he's simply *showing* them love so that they will show him love in return. After he's done "spreading love", he continues on his journey to find himself.

The more a man is in the company of a woman, the longer it will take him to find himself because for a man... a woman is often a great distraction. This is another reason why a man has to be *ready* for a relationship; he has to be able to afford the luxury of giving a woman his time, energy, and effort. A man who is lost can't afford to give a woman his time, energy, and effort because he'll get sidetracked from reaching his primary goals. Many times a woman will try to help a man find himself, but sometimes in order to help a man, you have to love him from a distance, so that he can stay focused. You are more powerful than you think, and you have to realize the power that you have over a man. If you want your man to stay focused, removing yourself from his presence will prove to be a very affective way to help.

No matter your gender, you have to love *yourself* before you can love someone else. This is why it's so important to get to know a person before getting emotionally involved. When a person doesn't love themselves, they're likely to subconsciously do things that hurt themselves, and if you're affiliated with that person, there's a great chance of them hurting you too. When a man doesn't love himself, it's still possible for him to care about others, but there's always the risk of him caring far less about others than he does for himself. When you meet a man who doesn't hold himself with high regards, you may want to step back and let him figure out who he wants to be on his *own* time.

When a man *shows* you his love, think short-term; you'll notice that he makes you feel special, makes you feel like you're the only one, but *only* when you're around. This means he could be doing the same exact thing with multiple different women on every day of the week. Knowing your role in a man's life is essential, and the way to figure out where you stand with a man is by getting to know him and coming to understand his morals and values system. There are many men who simply don't value honesty, family, and monogamy, so it's a great idea to know this upfront. You don't want a man to *loan* you his love, you want a man to *give* you his love, time, energy, and effort, and do so exclusively.

A man puts himself on the path of destruction when he lives a double life! Not only is he doing himself a disservice, but he's self-sabotaging the current relationship he's in, and at the same time, he's stunting his growth with the woman on the side. He hasn't found love for himself, so each time he makes an attempt to love another woman on the side, he'll be repeating the same cycle and hoping for different results; driving himself and every person involved insane. Some women don't require a man to hide his current relationship, but for the women who don't entertain such men, he'll have to somehow convince her that he is single, which is impossible to do in truth. He's developing stronger skills as a con artist and slowly but surely *becoming* his act.

Before a man can lie to a woman, he first has to lie to himself! He lies to himself by pretending to be honest, knowing that he's in fact being the total opposite. When a man starts a relationship off with a lie, this means he doesn't consider you to be someone he wants to be with in truth. Men primarily operate off of logic and reason, while women primarily operate off of love. Throughout a man's journey to find himself, he'll discover that love *has* no reason. Unconditional love isn't distributed evenly or easily, so when he finds that one woman who loves him unconditionally, he should hold onto her.

When a man *gives* you his love, think long-term. You'll know he loves you not by what he says, but by what he does! You'll also be able to tell if a man is *in* love with you by the things he *doesn't* do. When he refrains from doing things that would normally be acceptable during his single life, and cuts off certain people from his past, this is a great sign of a man's potential to be loyal. It's true that a man will say anything it takes to prove himself to a woman, but his actions will always speak far louder than his words. Never listen to a man's words... always follow his actions.

The things a man does for the woman he loves will never be duplicated for a woman on the side. A man of substance who knows who he is, knows where he's going, and knows what he wants for his life, values monogamy. He has too much invested in the woman and the life he has at home to entertain any other woman on the side. Sometimes women make the mistake of giving the same privileges to the man *in* the house as if he's the man *of* the house.

Just because a man is in your life, doesn't necessarily mean he wants to be a part of your life. Depending on where a man is in his life emotionally and financially, you may just be his *convenience*. If you're his convenience, he'll have no problem venturing off to another woman who he's more interested in. If he's the love of your life, and you're the love of his life, he will be a man of honor and prove to be an exclusive lover, a protector, and a provider.

Chapter Seven

Unspoken Truths About Men

Platonic Friendship Is An Oxymoron

All straight men have a motive! Straight men use "friendship" as a way to bring them closer to a woman and to possibly build a romantic relationship. They may pretend to be your friend, but in actuality, they're using a well thought out, planned strategy to get closer to your body. A man's agenda is to wait for as long as it takes until you're in your most vulnerable state so that you will finally be ready to do what he has always wanted to do from the start. While *you* may look at him as a "brother from another mother", the male on the other hand does not in any way shape or form view you as a sister, or even a friend for that matter. If you don't believe me, throw yourself at this "brother" of yours and watch how quickly he has sex with you.

A man might wait years or even a lifetime to declare his love or interest in a woman. This is all a part of his plan to successfully convince a woman into believing that it was the endless conversations about love & relationships, the constant interaction, and the desire to fill a void she's been missing that's driving him to suddenly confess his dying love. He's aware that in order to bring a woman's guards down, he has to be subtle and attack indirectly. He knows that friendship is the key to romance!

A man knows upon first sight whether he's interested in sleeping with a woman or not. A woman knows upon first sight whether or not she is interested in sleeping with a man or not. A man keeps in contact with a woman for one or more of the following reasons: Sex, money, resources. A woman keeps in contact with a man either because she secretly loves him, lusts him, or is using him for his resources. No matter your

188

gender, it's universally understood that no one associates closely with other people directly linked to their circle of trust for no reason.

Many women are convinced that a man's interest might die out if she tells him upfront that she's not romantically interested in him, or if years and years go by and nothing happens. Wrong!!! A man is well aware that going in for the kill too soon would ruin his plan to win you over. He has to wait for the right opportune moment. The moment where the move that he decides to make won't make you run away from him forever! We live in a visually oriented society, and men hand select women they want to closely associate with based on his initial sexual desire for her. A man's approach is pre-meditated with great hopes of having a sexual rendezvous at some point in the near future; not because he wants to solely be her "friend".

Once a man approaches you and gives you his million-dollar pick up line, it's up you to decide which direction you want the relationship to go in. His desire to sleep with you though will never go away. In fact, the only chance you have at reducing his interest in sleeping with you is by actually sleeping with him or perhaps gaining undesirable lbs. Otherwise, his desire to sleep with you will grow stronger and stronger after all of the time spent, all of the conversations, and all of the interactions. What you're experiencing through this platonic friendship is a false sense of security. He respects you just enough not to cross any lines and save face, but not enough to be a genuine friend.

He's your friend in a sense that friendship is the category that you placed him in, but in actuality, he's just another guy who would love to sleep with you, and *will* sleep with you if ever given the opportunity. This relationship that you have with this "male friend" will only grant you short-term victories, and you'll find this to be true when you experience limitations to his willingness to help/support you 100%. No one likes to feel used or abused, so choosing friends who can mutually benefit from being associated with you will prove to be of greater value to your life.

It will take a man of substance no time at all to figure out that his role in your life is to simply "be there" when you need him. A man who knows his worth will reserve doing anything for a woman who is willing to do anything for him! Since there is no room for potential romance between you two, the person you call on for favors should be a male relative, your partner, or whomever you're giving benefits to. Random men who show you favor will expect something in return and use their favors as "down payments". In other words "You owe me".

Your brother or a blood relative for example would be more willing to do things for you simply because you're related by blood, and even with that, his willingness to do things for you will have limits. A man who is "just a friend" doesn't have anything invested in you or vice versa, so his loyalty to you will depend on how close he thinks he's getting to you romantically. If this male friend of yours suddenly gets into in a relationship of his own, he will no longer be considered as *your* option because his priorities will have shifted to another woman. Being a priority is one of the benefits a woman gains by making a friend more than just a friend. The things he would normally do for you (while single) are now being done for a woman who has actually earned those privileges or is currently earning them through a "mutually beneficial arrangement".

If during this time you would like to call on this friend for a favor, you run the risk of causing turmoil in *his* relationship because his woman will view you as a potential threat. Any man who's in a committed relationship has no business doing another woman favors due to the emotional and psychological effect(s) it has on one or both parties (i.e. Sexual tension). His loyalty should remain to his woman exclusively. There even comes a time where even "Mom" gets told no (when it comes to his wife).

If you closely associate with a man who's romantically interested in you, be sure to consider the costs that come along with this association. If you're mutually interested in him, by all means, spend as much time as you'd like with him. If you're not mutually interested in him, know that if you closely associate with him, it's only a matter of time before he makes a sexual advance through his actions or his words. It's the law of attraction and it should never be ignored. Be aware… be smart… be safe!

"Best Friends" Want To Become Sex Friends

Some men have a hard time expressing their *true* feelings for many reasons; one of these reasons is their fear of rejection. It's quite common for a man to lose a woman's trust after expressing to her that he wants *more* than a platonic friendship. To avoid rejection or ruining what she feels is a *platonic* friendship; he (for the time being) accepts his role as a friend and uses it as a smokescreen. He's well aware that friendship is the foundation that helps build successful relationships; however, he's not giving *you* the opportunity to decide whether you'd like to remain associated with him after discovering his romantic interest in you. Instead he's giving you a *false* sense of security, and doesn't seem to have a problem with doing so.

It's likely that the woman is *genuinely* interested in only having a friendship as it gives her a sense of *companionship* without being romantically involved, however the *male* has other plans in mind. No man in his right mind is going to wait months, or years for a woman to see value in him and give him a chance. No man of substance, who has a high level of confidence and esteem, is going to wait months or years to express his love towards a woman. Any man who's not confident enough to approach a woman and tell her how he truly feels is a *coward*, and the last thing you want is a coward leading your household or your family anyway. You want a man who's able to take charge and take control over any and every situation. The same men you feel may look at you as a sister are the same ones who have a *strong* desire to be a love interest; he's simply waiting for the right time and the right way to tell you.

A man can go to his boys if he just wants to hang out and have a good time just for the hell of it. When a man associates with a woman it's because he's hoping to get closer to her body. Life and relationships are like a game of chess; you study your target, plan your moves, and always keep your mate in check. For a *male friend*, playing chess is his best bet if he wants to get closer to a woman. Oh yes, he knows exactly what he's doing when he sits and listens to your guy troubles, comes and gives you a lift when you've gotten a flat tire, or loans you money when you're behind on bills. All of these things aren't being done simply out of the goodness of his heart; every last one of these gestures are *down payments*. They're a sign of good faith showing you that he's a good man; one that you should consider for more than just a friend.

Sometimes based on certain circumstances, the friend zone is the only place that he can be and still remain *close*. You might currently be in a relationship with someone, so that means he can't directly approach you or show interest, so he'll remain a supportive friend and "pick up the pieces" whenever you and your boyfriend are having relationship troubles. Or he might be in a relationship himself, and he'll refer to you as a "friend" just to keep you around and also to make his woman feel secure. When a man is in a relationship, acting as a friend will seem so *sincere*, but really what's happening is it's the only *safe* approach for him to take (for the time being).

A straight man has no desire to be "just friends" with a woman. When it comes to females, men use friendship as a way to get closer to a woman for personal gain (i.e. sex, money, or resources). They want the warmth and the comfort of a woman, and they want that from *you* either short-term or long-term. A quality man of substance won't have the time or the patience to spend months or years pursuing a woman in hopes for a relationship. At most, he'll stick around that long solely for the opportunity to sleep with you, but nothing more. He understands that if a woman isn't genuinely interested from the beginning, not to expect anything different in the end.

     A man's sexual interest in a woman never dies (unless something has drastically changed in her physical appearance). Otherwise, no matter how many years pass by, he will always be ready, willing, and available for sex whenever you are. A man who holds himself with high-esteem will more than likely view you as someone who took him for granted and didn't see the value in him for all these years. So if you give yourself to *this* particular man, he'll gladly have sex with you, but nothing further will transpire. His pride won't let you have the glory.

     On the other hand, the man with low self-esteem who's been literally chasing you for the entire duration of your friendship will *gladly* consider you for a relationship and overlook the reality that he was never a *first* option… and is now a *last* resort. He's desperate and he's not ashamed of it. If you didn't see anything in him when you first met him, or throughout the years you've known each other, don't convince yourself that he miraculously is that man for you *now*. Once you give yourself to him, he will do any and everything in his power to keep you, almost in an overbearing, controlling, *clingy* kind of way. Enter *this* relationship at your own risk.

Platonic friendship is an oxymoron, and *all* men have a motive. If he chose you to be his friend, he'll *gladly* choose you for sex. You're not obligated to entertain any of their proposals, but it's in your best interest to identify *who* these men are, and govern yourself accordingly. Ignoring these truths will only ruin what you thought was a great friendship, or may even cause trouble in your relationship with your man. Always trust and believe that all men have a motive.

Men Don't Want Sloppy Seconds

Finding someone who's pure and untouched in this day and age is possible, but rare. In today's times, we expect our significant other to have *some* kind of history, but even still we don't want to knowingly be associated with the men from your past, no matter how long ago it was. One of the major aspects that go into choosing a girlfriend or wife is the idea of being with someone who is *exclusive* (meaning none of the men *we* know have had you or *can* have you). There's also a *code of honor* amongst men, and that code is you don't commit to a woman that one of your friends or relatives used to be sexually involved with. It's a conflict of interest!

There are millions of women in the world, and the last thing a man would want to do is settle on a woman who one of his close friends has the drop on. He wants his friends to have respect for the woman he's with, and he also wants the assurance of knowing that any men who are in his circle of friends have never had the privilege of seeing his woman naked. Yes, it's a matter of *pride*! After all, you do want your man to be proud of the woman he's with, right?

There are a lot of women out there who *always* dress provocatively, or work in a sex related industry and can't quite figure out why they're struggling in the *love* department. Part of the reason is because they're not showing that they're capable of being *exclusive*. They have this burning desire to be seen, heard, and at the center of attention by a multitude of men, and *that* goes against the exclusivity of a relationship. The other reason is that since *they* don't seem to value their bodies, the men who approach them are looking to either exploit their bodies even further, or experience their bodies for themselves. *Love* has nothing to do with *these* men's reasoning for the pursuit. *This* pursuit is strictly sex driven; and because he doesn't value her from the beginning, he'll never truly look to value her in the end.

For a man, it's a conflict of interest to entertain a woman who doesn't value herself enough to have standards and set requirements. A person's past is a reflection of their character, and a person's character influences the decisions they make in *life*. Men are very proud individuals; *so* proud that they can't and won't endure the thought of being with a woman who degraded herself in the past or slept with someone he knows. There's no sense in lying to a man about your past, because if he's genuinely interested in you, he's going to do a *thorough* background check on you just to make sure he's not committing to a whore.

A man who's interested in having a future with you will protect your honor, but only if you're doing the same for yourself. Most men associate closely with other men who reflect who *they* are as a person; so naturally, they'll have similar taste in women, and similar ways that they treat women. Knowing that you've entertained his friend is *enough* detail for him to imagine the type of relationship that you and his friend might've had. Once he gets wind that the two of you were intimate, those thoughts will constantly be in the forefront of his mind and he won't be able to get over it.

It's easy for a man to choose a woman to *sleep* with; all he has to do is look for the woman who matches his physical taste. When it comes to choosing a girlfriend or a wife however, he looks for a woman using his eyes *and* his heart. This means that your personality & your character are at the forefront and your physical beauty becomes an added bonus. If you're ever faced with a situation where the man you're dating is friends with an old flame of yours, make the judgment call early on and decide if it's even worth pursuing. Being forthcoming and honest about this sort of thing could potentially save the both of you a world of emotional damage. He might not be able to entertain the relationship further than sex, but he *will* respect you for considering his feelings.

If you honestly and truly want to be in a happy, loving, long lasting relationship with someone, choose a man who's not connected to any of the men in your past. There are too many negatives to consider when pursuing someone who's closely associated with an old flame and frankly it's not worth the trouble. The last thing you want is to be tormented and/or constantly reminded of your past by your significant other. Take this time to focus on what's relevant in *your* life, and when the right man comes along, be proud to share the story of your life with him.

Hurt Men, Hurt Women

A man doesn't know love until he meets a woman. Since a woman births a man, his life automatically begins with a *sample* of what love is! The unconditional love found between a mother and a son is not a relationship that everyone has the privilege of experiencing, however when this special bond is present, it heavily influences the way a son looks at his mother, which in turn affects the way he looks at women as a whole. The bond between a loving mother and son is unconditional, knows no limits, and has no end.

A son's mother is his "First Lady", and the relationship between the two of them (or the lack thereof) will explain a great deal of his behaviors towards women throughout life! A mother loves him, nurtures him, feeds him, clothes him, protects him, and would even die for him. When in the presence of his mother, a man feels safe, secure; the connection between the two is physical, emotional, and spiritual. Being in the presence of a mother who is loving and nurturing is where a man feels he is most comfortable and vulnerable and his desire in life is to find a woman who also has this special power!

Upon seeking a woman who is comparable to his mother, a man's love path can be significantly influenced and/or manipulated. One of the most love altering influences in a man's life is the presence of another male. While a mother primarily influences her son with matters of the heart, a father primarily influences his son with matters pertaining to the mind and the body! The love that a man shows a woman is considered unusual when expressed towards another male, and this behavior is almost always rejected.

A father (or male influences) teaches a young boy how to be "tough", how to "be a man", how to be a "protector" and a "provider". A man communicates with another man through his actions; he uses his words as a last resort in the event that his actions haven't clearly conveyed a message. The way that a man handles another man is no way for a man to handle a woman. It is the relationship that the father has with the sons' mother, and the relationship that the son has with his mother that gives men the blueprint for acceptable behavior with a woman.

When a father is instrumental in a son's life, a son uses the knowledge and skills acquired from this trusted source. When the father is not present or not instrumental, a man uses the male influences of the world (i.e. Men in the neighborhood, men in school, men at work, celebrity profiles on TV, etc). No matter where he gets his teachings from, a man will have a strong desire to put these lessons to the test. The approach will differ depending on his influences, but his goal remains the same; he wants to be loved!

Character reflects one's behavior; one's behavior is influenced by one's upbringing and surrounding influences. We have no control over who births us, who raises us, or who influences us, but no matter who we are and where we're from, as humans we all want to be loved. Since a man is trained by other men to wear armor around his heart, he looks for a woman whom will allow him to finally put his guards down.

Think of it as a game of "Are you my mother?" Men are constantly in search of a woman who reminds him of his mother. First, he must see a woman of interest with his eyes, and then he must feel a woman of interest with his heart, and then connect on a spiritual level. Before a spiritual connection can be made, he has to build up the courage that his father instilled in him and say "Hello, my name is…". If the love that he shows this woman is reciprocated, this could possibly be the end of his love search! If the love that he shows this woman is rejected, this could be his very first experience with heartbreak from a woman outside of the home.

A man who is showered with love from his mother grows to also become loving to other women. His loving/nurturing nature is instilled in his mind, body and soul. Due to the relationship he has with his mother (1st Lady), "rejection" from a woman is an uncommon reaction that causes pain and builds up resentment. This is one of many possible rejection clauses that might influence what would've been a potentially good man to mistreat women.

Don't let a man's exterior fool you; Men are hard on the outside, but extremely soft on the inside. A mother is a man's escape from the dark, cruel, cold, hard world, but as an adult, he looks to find this escape with a woman he can call his own! This world is a cold, dark, and lonely place to be if you're a man, which is why a man will endlessly look for a woman to shine her light, brighten his day, and add warmth to his life.

Each time a man is rejected, it feels like a knife takes a stab to his heart and causes emotional damage. Society isn't aware of these emotionally setbacks because he's wearing his protective armor so that he can appear strong, tough, and independent! And he is indeed strong, tough, and independent, but this guard often poses a problem when it comes to being "vulnerable" to a woman. Being rejected so frequently by jobs, social clubs, and women causes a man to become emotionally unavailable and shut down that part of him.

Rejection is motivation to become better at being accepted, but not every man has totally accessed this level of power! In the event that a job, social club, or a woman that previously had rejected him later accepts him, the initial resentment caused by being rejected will still remain. This "attitude" will cause him to seek revenge for the emotional distress he experienced when he was rejected. When a person is used to being treated with love, nurture and care, experiencing the opposite causes a disturbance in one's peace of mind.

Women are a source of love, but not every woman is ready and willing to give it. When a man approaches a woman, his desire is to receive love (on one level or another). Based on his upbringing, he may or may not know exactly what to say, how to say it, or what steps to take in order to continue to be in the favor of a woman romantically. By being rejected, he then learns what doesn't work, but he continues to live his life not knowing what does. In addition, this new rejection will add to the resentment he's built up and stored in his heart towards women.

With countless male influences always available, his new advised approach will more than likely be to work on his physique, his finances, and his material goods (i.e. Swag). Swag will get the women, but a good heart will keep her. Matters of the heart aren't a conversation that a man typically has with another man. The less female influence a male has, the less he will understand what it takes to get and keep a woman. The more female influences a male has, the more he will understand what it takes to get and keep a woman. As a positive solution to male-to-female interaction, we must communicate with one another in efforts to help build happier/healthier relationships.

With communication comes understanding, respect, and reverence for one another. By opening the door of communication you welcome the opportunity for friendship, companionship, and love. By closing the door of communication, you leave enemies, burned bridges, and hate waiting on the outside! Every human deserves to be treated with dignity and respect. Never allow your emotional state to negatively affect someone else's. Be consistent with loving yourself and everyone else.

The Reason Why Men Cheat

Cheating isn't gender specific; it starts in a person's heart, not in their pants. A cheater will cheat no matter what they have at home. A person's decision to be disloyal has less to do with *you*, than it does with what's going on inside of *them*; it's a disease (if you will). It's a disease that can only be cured by maturity, growth, and perhaps a good taste of their own medicine. Often times we find ourselves in situations where we're unhappy, and we desperately want to find a solution to the problem. A man of substance will take the high road and talk to his partner about it, or leave the relationship, while a man of poor character will take the low road and "outsource". There is no excuse for cheating and there is no one to blame but one's self for doing so; cheating shows a lack of respect for the relationship and shouldn't be taken lightly.

Whether things are going well in the relationship or not, if your man makes the decision to cheat, his actions don't indicate that it's *you* that's making him cheat, his actions show that *he* lacks integrity, is dishonest, disloyal, selfish, and has no respect for himself, you, or the relationship. Cheating is a huge reflection of one's character. You can get a pretty good idea of a man's character based on a number of things (i.e. The place you met him and under what circumstances, the company he keeps, his upbringing, his male influences, his relationship with his parents, his experience in his past relationships, just to name a few).

It's important that you take the time to truly get to know a man before you allow yourself to get *too* emotionally attached. The signs of a cheater are in fact

204

more easily identifiable than you think; you simply have to know what signs to look for. Ideally, you'll have to get to know a man's *heart* to be certain. The average cheater has an abundance of options, and if he is not reached a high level of maturity, he will without a doubt *entertain* those options. Always remember that relationships aren't for everybody, relationships are for the *ready*; a person who cheats clearly isn't ready to be in a committed relationship.

Plainly put... cheaters are *spoiled*; they want what they want when they want it, and they won't have it any other way. They're opportunist and they love the idea of trying new things, experiencing new thrills, and living for the moment! You've seen a spoiled child in action when he doesn't get his way; he'll go and do *something* to compensate for the attention the parent isn't giving him. It's not that the parent doesn't love the child, it's not that the parent doesn't provide the child with everything he needs, it's simply that the child wants *more*! The same theory applies to grown men; he could have the *best* woman and the *best* life at home, but because he is never satisfied, he has to go out and seek *more*!

If a man cheats on you once, it's because *he* allowed it to happen. If a man cheats on you twice, it's because *you* allowed it to happen. Once a man shows you that he doesn't respect *himself*, you can't expect him to treat *you* any better. Cheating is the ultimate sign of disrespect, and it should not go without consequences. Once you take a cheater back, you're letting him know that no matter what he does, he will always be welcome back home.

One thing women have to realize is that men are

master strategists; he may not be the best at hiding things, but he is a master at implementing them. Anything a man wants in life, he will go after, and he will achieve it if he puts his mind to it. When a man seeks out a woman, he strategizes; he evaluates himself and where he's at financially, emotionally, and spiritually, and then he targets women whose esteem is low enough to accept him in his current state. What this means is, if he's a man of poor character, he's going to bypass women of substance because *he's* not anyone of substance. He instead is going to *target* a woman whom he knows will settle for just *any* man, just so long as he doesn't appear to be someone that could hurt her.

It's sad when a woman takes a man back from cheating, because they don't quite understand that he was planning on cheating on you before he even met you. Maybe I can put it in another way... he never planned on being loyal to you in the *first* place; you were merely a stepping-stone in his life. When a man is finally ready to settle down, he will have gotten all the promiscuity out of his system and will be ready for something *more*! As a woman, you have to know and understand *when* a man is ready, but more importantly when he is not. Many times the sex can be *so* good that a man will hold onto you *just* to have easy access to unlimited sex.

Some men agree to relationships just so that no one else can have access to you; it's a selfish move, but this is what *a lot* men do. Meanwhile, as you wait at home twiddling your thumbs, he's out screwing any and everything moving. You were set up for failure from the very beginning. Maybe it was your dangerous curves, mind-blowing sex, your loaded bank account, or your ability to get him exposure in a particular field that caught his attention, but whatever it was, it wasn't *love* if he's disrespecting you. This is why it's extremely important to properly get to know a person because it grants you the opportunity to measure what it is he values, and to also see if he truly values *you*.

When it comes to cheaters, all he needs is a *reason*, and that will be all the fuel he needs to be disloyal. There is no way to avoid being cheated on, but you can avoid allowing him to be a repeat offender. Know your worth and don't settle for a man who blatantly disrespects you and your relationship. By standing your ground and letting him know that you will not tolerate his behavior, you regain your position of power, and you also gain his respect. Nothing hurts a man more than being left by a woman, so if he hurts you by cheating, you can return the favor by walking away.

Men Can Dish It, But Can't Take It

Anytime a man cheats, it's time for you to reevaluate the relationship. Cheating lets you know that whatever it is you're doing isn't enough to satisfy him. There's nothing you can do about it and if you take him back once, he will without a doubt cheat again. Cheaters don't play fair, and after everything's said and done you'll never be able to fully trust him again after he's proven to be disloyal. If your partner cheats, the contract is breached!

A cheater wants to have *more* than everyone else, and the only way for him to ensure that he's getting more than you is to live a double life behind your back. If he entertained other women in your face, that would reveal his hidden agenda and might prompt you to even the playing field. He's not looking for an open relationship, no! He's looking for a one-sided relationship where he gets to do whatever he wants to do, while you're sitting at home being loyal. He could very easily be single and play the field but no, he would much rather drag you through the mud while he plays instead.

When a cheater gets away with cheating, he considers this to be "winning"! He's having his cake and eating it too while no one suspects a thing. This may be loads of fun for him, but it's disrespectful to you, your family, his family, your friends, and anyone else who might also have been a witness to his lies and deceit. Cheaters lack *integrity* so don't expect them to come clean if you accuse them of cheating, and don't expect them to be forthcoming either. The thrill for him is in *hiding* the truth, not *telling* the truth.

Anytime a cheater gets caught cheating, he

won't be sorry about the cheating, no! He's sorry that he got *caught*, and now he's looking for a way out of the mess *he* created. Even still, after being caught cheating you'll notice that he *still* isn't being considerate of your feelings. He'll say he's sorry, beg, plead, promise to never do it again, and he may even be bold enough to deny the whole thing. Instead of giving you time to reflect on what just happened, he'd smother you and try to force you into buying into his lies and deceit. He'll expect you to immediately take him back without giving it any thought whatsoever because he's only considering his own feelings and not yours.

Now let the tables turn and imagine that you stepped out and cheated on him just *one* time; he is going to LOSE HIS MIND! He won't be able to wrap his mind around how you could possibly do such a thing to him, even after the many times he's done it to you. His pride and ego might even force him to leave you without even thinking twice about it because this time, he's been beaten at his own game. If he stays, you'll never hear the end of it, and he'll drive you crazy with his constant questioning of your whereabouts and his insecurity. Part of the reason for his insecurity is that he's still cheating. The other part is that he's afraid that you're going to beat him to the punch and he doesn't want you to have your cake and it too just like he did.

Cheaters cheat because they don't appreciate the value in being *fair* and they've grown so accustomed to cutting corners, scamming others, and burning bridges that it's become a part of their everyday make-up. Sometimes in order for a man to humble himself, he has to hit rock bottom. It's unfortunate, but *some* men need

Food, Sex & Peace of Mind

a little help and need to be *crushed* to help them reach that bottom. Once they've experienced a taste of their own medicine, they'll get a feel of what it's like to be heartbroken, to feel betrayed, and to be disrespected by someone they love.

Cheating should never be a solution for anyone in a relationship; if you're unhappy, simply talk to your partner about it and come up with the best possible solution. No one deserves to be lied to, deceived, or betrayed, even if it was done to him or her first! There's no telling what an emotionally charged man with a bruised ego might do to you if he found out that you were cheating, and you don't want to find out! You only have one life to live, so protect yourself at all cost! If you or your partner feels the need to outsource, talk to one another instead and consider the possibility of either making the relationship work, or moving on and living single.

Acknowledgments

First I would like to Thank God for giving me the strength, courage, and wisdom to write this book. Second I want to thank my mother for being such an amazing woman, and instilling great family values in me. To my brothers Joshua, Shane, Travis (@OmegaDaDon), and Milton, and my step-brother Aaron, I love you and I appreciate everything that I've been able to learn from you guys.

Thank you Coach Bob Hurley for the priceless values you've instilled in me when I was a high school student/athlete; hard work, dedication, and discipline certainly pays off. Thank you Paul C. Brunson (@PaulCBrunson) for being a great motivator and inspiring me with your great words of wisdom. Big thanks to Sonia Carroll (@SoniaCarroll) for helping with editing/revising my book. Thank you Joseph Buapim (@Jbdesigns1 @ignmagazine) for designing my book cover.

To my two best friends Kerry Neal (@KDotZilla) and Khayri McKinney (@KmcKinney1424), you already KNOW!!! I love you guys and we're going to do some amazing things for the youth in our communities. The 3 of us graduated together, partied together, talked endlessly about women and relationships and now I've finally put it in a book before you guys did! Lol. We've had some of the best experiences EVER and I wouldn't trade it for the world! You were all a part of my motivation to write this book.

My sister Jordi (@Jordstyle) gets her own

paragraph! Jordi, you are the best sister a brother could ever have and I'm glad you're mine. You've taught me *so* much about men, women, relationships, and business long before you even knew I was listening. You're fun, loving, caring, smart, beautiful, a great listener, innovative thinker, and I honestly and truly don't know where I'd be without you. You've been there for me when I needed you the most and you've always believed in my visions and ideas. Not only did you believe in me, but you've also invested in me and I love you for it! You're not just my sister, but you're my best *female* friend ;)

AskCheyB wouldn't exist without an audience! Thank you to each and every one of you who took the time to email me your questions for enlightenment and empowerment. Thank you to everyone who subscribed to my YouTube channel for relationship advice. Thank you to everyone who added me on Facebook, liked my relationship posts, and commented on the daily discussions. Thank you to everyone who follows me on Twitter, RT's, and interacts with me, and also a big thank you to everyone who reads and subscribes to my relationship blog.

Last but not least, I would like to thank all of the women from my past. You've been a great source of inspiration for this book. Thank you! :*

50 Inspirational Quotes from Chey B.

The fastest way to eliminate a problem is to address it!

If you're looking for love… hold up a mirror!

You can't move onto the next… until you're through with your ex!

If love and happiness can be found inside of you… you'll never go a day without it!

Be *independent* when you're single and *interdependent* when you're in a relationship.

Once you stop loving, you'll start hating. Once you stop hating, you'll start loving!

Command respect from the beginning, so you won't have to demand respect in the end!

Never listen to a man's *words*. Always follow his *actions*!

Your dependents are your children, not your partner!

Friendship should be the beginning, not the end!

Avoid people who bring out the worst in you. Embrace those who bring out the best in you!

When you carry yourself like you're somebody, people are less likely to treat you like you're nobody!

Food, Sex & Peace of Mind

If your partner cheats, the contract is breached!

A man will *say* anything to get you into bed, but he'll only *do* what you require!

When it comes to your network, you have to remove the people who are harmful & add the people who are helpful.

Sex is something that a man you're not married to should be able to look *forward* to, not look *back* upon.

Giving is about what you put forth, not what you get back!

Forgiving isn't about what it does for someone else, it's about what it does for "you"!

Your outer beauty is what will get a man to come; your inner beauty is what will get a man to stay.

Your worth is determined by the value you add to the lives of *others*.

Being single is the thing you do when you're establishing/finding yourself and/or when you haven't yet met someone who meets your standards.

It's impossible to achieve your goals if you don't set any!

If your best friend isn't your boyfriend, he should be promoted. If your boyfriend isn't your best friend, he

214

should be demoted!

Being single is the best place to be when the person you were with didn't make a good double!

If you know your worth, show your worth!

Never consider those who never consider you!

If you're living your life, you're not worried about what someone else is doing! If you're worried about what someone else is doing, you're not living your life!

Focus on your education, your career, your health, your happiness. Focus on a man when he focuses on you.

Staying in a bad relationship hurts you. Leaving a bad relationship hurts him!

Money can only buy you things that are for sale. Love has never been on the market and it never will be!

Your past relationships were only a waste of time if you didn't learn anything from them!

The only way to get a man to stop cheating on you is by leaving him!

When you were in a relationship, you were busy doing "y'all". Now that you're single, get busy doing "you"!

Not everything in life will be logical or practical. Some things are done simply out of "Love"; Love has no reason!

Do the right thing… so people can always use that against you!

Never *look* for a relationship, but always prepare yourself to be ready for one!

You can't do anything to control your child's life… but you can do everything to influence it!

Work on being the best person you can be and you'll attract the best people.

Sex is a great way to keep a man in your bed, but it's no way to keep a man in your life!

If a person doesn't see value in you from the beginning, that should be the end!

It's essential never to commit to "potential".

Go where you're celebrated, not tolerated!

If the person you're with is constantly breaking your heart... Learn your lesson and stop giving it to them!

The best way to remain a couple is to do things *as* a couple!

Always present yourself as the person you want to be known and remembered as!

Finding yourself means you're not looking for others.

Who you *are,* is not who you *were.* Who you *are,* is who you've become "after" being who you were!

Allow life to take you places... Not keep you places!

It's easy to get into a relationship, but if you don't have the tools that make a relationship work, you'll be lost when things need fixing.

Two people should know your worth; you, and the person who wants to be a part of you.

25927679R00136

Made in the USA
Lexington, KY
09 September 2013